They Sank the Red Dragon

Oswald Frederick Swayne.

They Sank the Red Dragon

Bernard Edwards

Cardiff
1987

GPC Books is an imprint of University of Wales Press, 6 Gwennyth Street, Cardiff, CF2 4YD

© Bernard Edwards, 1987

British Library Cataloguing in Publication Data
Edwards, Bernard
    They sank the Red Dragon.
    1. World War, 1939–1945——Naval operations,
    British 2. Merchant ships——Wales——
    History——20th century
    I. Title
    940.54'59429   D770

ISBN 0–7083–0966–6

Printed at The Bath Press, Avon

for Oswald Frederick Swayne and the men
of the Welsh ships who gave their lives

Unrecognised; you put us in your debt;
Unthanked, you enter or escape the grave;
Whether your land remember or forget
You saved the land, or died to try to save.

John Masefield, For All Seafarers.

Contents

Illustrations

Preface

The basis of this book is factual, being taken from reports by survivors, convoy commodores and escort commanders, held in the Public Record Office in London. However, these chronicles are, in the main, terse and self-effacing and required some carefully researched elaboration to reveal the full story. I have also, in some cases, attempted to enter the minds of the central characters, interpreting their unwritten thoughts, hopes and fears in the light of my own experience in merchant ships. In no case have I set out to weave a deliberate web of fantasy but, if I have at times paraphrased too liberally, then I crave the indulgence of those concerned.

Bernard Edwards
Llanvaches, Gwent.
1986

Acknowledgements

The author gratefully acknowledges the help given to him in the research for this book by the following sources and people:

Public Record Office, Kew; General Register & Record Office of Shipping & Seamen, Llandaff; Welsh Industrial & Maritime Museum, Cardiff; Central Reference Library, Newport; Bundesarchiv, Koblenz; Captain R. Newbury, Department of Transport, Cardiff; J. Geraint Jenkins and David Jenkins, Welsh Industrial & Maritime Museum; Ted Goddard, Western Telegraph; Captain T. C. Rooney, Nautical Institute; Harold Appleyeard, World Ship Society; Horst-Arthur Lange, Hamburg; Oberst-Leutnant Horst Muller, Cologne; George Swayne, Desmond Swayne, Adeline Fuller (née Swayne), Violet Ley (née Swayne), Captain Byron Davies, Haven Puxley, Nicola Waters.

The publishers would like to acknowledge the following for their kind permission to reproduce the illustrations contained in this book: Desmond Swayne; Welsh Industrial and Maritime Museum; A. Duncan; Bundesarchiv, Koblenz; Imperial War Museum, London.

1

Prelude to war

History records Christopher Columbus as being the first man to sail across the Atlantic to the Americas. Welsh legend will have it Prince Madoc preceded the Genoese by 322 years. Again, evidence recently unearthed points to the Welsh mariner John Lloyd also having made the long crossing in 1477, fifteen years before Columbus set sail. Whatever the truth of this much argued matter, the seamen of Wales cannot be denied their place in the forefront of the annals of British maritime accomplishment. Henry Morgan, Howell Davis and Bartholomew Roberts may have been somewhat dishonest in their procurement of cargoes, but they were seamen cast in a mould long since broken. During the latter half of the nineteenth century, the coastal villages of Wales were home to battalions of Cape Horners; men who would run a square-rigger around the world before a hurricane, ever grumbling at the lack of wind. Close on their heels, in the ugly age of steam, came the Welsh tramp-ship men, adept at operating on the thinnest of shoestrings, but never lowering their professional standards an inch. They, without doubt, were the best in a world of hard, courageous seamen.

The great boom in Welsh shipping began in the 1880s with a world-wide demand for Welsh steam coal, considered the best fuel for the ships, factories and railways of the new steam revolution. At this time, a new breed of entrepreneurial shipowners moved into Wales, many of them originating in the West Country and the Channel Islands. There were fortunes to be made and made they were. Cardiff, gateway to the South Wales valleys, thick with coalfields and pulsating iron mills, became the centre of this bustling maritime progression. At the outbreak of the First World War, more than 120 separate shipping companies had their offices in the Welsh capital, most of them in the Bute Street area. Men like William Reardon Smith from Bideford, Henry Radcliffe of Merthyr Tydfil, William James Tatem from Appledore, Philip and Thomas Morel from the Channel Islands and John Cory of Padstow were in the van of this great enterprise. They built their ships on the North-East coast of England, where lay some of the world's finest shipbuilding expertise. They were basic ships, cheap to build and economical to run, but eminently seaworthy and long-lasting. They were tramp steamers.

A tramp steamer is all that its name implies. In contrast to the cargo liner, which runs on a scheduled, advertised service, the tramp wanders from port to port, offering its services to the highest bidder, prepared to carry any cargo anywhere. It is usually a box-shaped ship, giving maximum cargo capacity for draught, low powered to avoid excessive fuel consumption and with crew accommodation offering only the bare necessities required for eating, sleeping and protection from the elements. In the case of the Welsh tramps of the first half of this century, their staple cargo outward was, of course, South Wales coal, returning home with grain, ore, timber or similar low-freight homogeneous cargoes. In between, if the opportunity was there, they would shuttle as many as half a dozen cargoes to and from ports outside the United Kingdom, often being away from home for a year at a time.

Many of the men who manned the Welsh tramps were drawn from West Wales, from Pembrokeshire and Cardiganshire, where a vast reservoir of experienced master mariners and seamen existed. It was not unusual for the entire crew of a ship, from Master down to deck boy, to hail from the same village, bringing with them the customs, prejudices and aspirations of their community ashore. Their common origin and religion were strong bonds, making for a tight and efficient ship. 'Cleanliness Next to Godliness' has long been the watchword in the West, so it is not surprising the Welsh tramps were renowned for their bright paintwork. The machinery of many of them, however, was often in a dubious state of repair.

In those tranquil days before the hordes of cost-cutting accountants put their dead hands to the throats of commerce, most British shipping companies were family businesses. The Welsh shipowner, in particular, although demanding his pound of flesh at all times, felt a strong responsibility for his employees, often looking on them as an integral part of his family. He took a genuine interest in his ships, visiting them in person whenever possible, listening to complaints and suggestions, often involving himself in the personal lives of his men, most of whom he knew by name. In return for this compassion shown by their employers, the men of the Welsh ships gave hard work, honesty and a fierce loyalty. It was a far cry from today, when there is so often an unbridgeable chasm between a faceless owner and his ships.

When the industrialized world ran into the worst slump in its history in the late 1920s, the coal trade was hard hit, resulting in a severe thinning of the ranks of the Welsh shipowners. By 1930, there were only seventy-seven shipping companies with offices in Cardiff, with just over 300 ships on their books. The smallest and weakest had gone but the big names were now firmly established. Sir William Reardon Smith & Sons, Evan Thomas, Radcliffe & Co., South American Saint Line, Tatem Steam Navigation Co., Graig Shipping, Constants (South Wales) and a handful of others were household names in the shipping world. By 1939, Welsh shipping had slimmed down to a mere twenty or so companies, with 164 ships of around 750,000 tons between them. Some of these ships were singularly un-Welsh at first glance, being registered in London or, in the case of Reardon Smith, in Bideford. The names, too, were confusing, Tatems prefering to call their ships after the Devonian towns ending with the suffix 'leigh', as in *Hadleigh* and *Everleigh*; Morels used Channel Island names, while Reardon Smith had a preference for American cities. The manning pattern had also changed, with an influx of English, Scots and Irish into the ships. However, with a hard core of Welsh

masters and seamen, and being firmly based in the South
Wales ports, the ships had lost none of their Welsh identity.
They were to play a vital part in the events of the years to
follow.

Being an island with limited natural resources, Britain is
largely dependent on her merchant shipping for her survival
and prosperity. She cannot hope to exist for long without food
for her population, oil for her transport and raw materials
for her manufacturing industries. This weakness was magnified
tenfold during the Second World War, when Britain could
never have been anything more than a transient bulwark of
Western democracy without substantial aid from her dominions and the United States of America. Her merchant fleet
was therefore her maritime jugular, stretched tight and often
dangerously exposed. From the first hours of the outbreak of
the war, the Axis powers, led by Britain's old naval adversary,
Germany, took their sharpened knives to the pulsating vein.

The men of Britain's Merchant Navy, although unarmed
civilians going about their normal business, were the first to
be involved in the war against Nazi Germany. Less than nine
hours after the declaration of war at 11 am on 3 September
1939, the Donaldson liner *Athenia* was sunk without warning
by a U-boat off the west coast of Ireland. From that moment
onwards, British merchant seamen were constantly in the front
line in all quarters of the globe. For almost six years they
faced, without flinching, their own private hell of torpedoes,
bombs, shells and mines, all the while fending off their old
arch-enemy the sea. Sorely pressed, and often tired near to
death, they kept open Britain's tenuous lifelines, bringing in
millions of tons of raw materials, food, arms and ammunition,
without which the country could not have survived. As always,
their spirit was indomitable, their professionalism unchallenged. The price they paid for their bravery and dedication
was horrific; 2,426 ships of 11,331,933 tons lost, 29,180 men
killed.

Since Prince Madoc first crossed the North Atlantic, this
turbulent ocean has been an accursed place in the eyes of

those who must sail it in pursuit of a living. It is a cold, unfriendly sea, often scourged by the most violent of storms; seldom at rest. In winter, each swirling depression follows so closely on the heels of the other that they merge to give an area of 4 million square miles of angry water, constantly seething beneath a low canopy of sombre grey cloud, unbroken from horizon to horizon. In summer, the storms are muted and sporadic, but foolish is the seaman who would ignore their menace. It was on such a battlefield that the fiercest actions of the war at sea were fought. Here the ships of the Red Dragon, many of them traditional Western Ocean traders, took their heaviest losses. Of the 123 Welsh ships lost in the war, 90 of them were sunk in the North Atlantic.

Winston Churchill was to write in later years: 'The Battle of the Atlantic was the dominating factor all through the war. Never for one moment could we forget that everything happening elsewhere, on land, at sea, or in the air, depended ultimately on its outcome, and amid all other cares we viewed its changing fortunes day by day with hope or apprehension. Many gallant actions and incredible feats of endurance are recorded, but the deeds of those who perished will never be known. Our merchant seamen displayed their highest qualities, and the brotherhood of the sea was never more strikingly shown than in their determination to defeat the U-boat.'

For almost four years the battle did not go well for the merchant ships, scarcity of escorts and indifferent air-cover making the fight hopelessly one-sided. The German type VII-C U-boats, of which 650 were thrown into the conflict, had a range of 8,500 miles, carried 14 torpedoes, an 88 mm deck gun and 3 anti-aircraft cannons, and were capable of maximum speeds of 17.3 knots on the surface and 7.6 knots submerged. Against them for much of the time were ranged tiny 900-ton Flower class corvettes of the Royal Navy, with a top speed of 15 knots and armed with a single 4-inch gun and a handful of depth charges. Attacking on the surface at night, the U-boats were able to out-gun and out-manouver these brave little ships.

In the early stages of the war, there had been a gap of 1,700 miles in mid-Atlantic, where the merchant ships, huddled together in convoy like nervous cattle, were beyond the range of the Royal Navy escorts stationed on either side of the Atlantic. It was here the most grievous slaughter took place, the unopposed U-boats falling upon the helpless merchantmen like packs of slavering wolves. Yet, despite the terrible losses they suffered, the convoys always clawed their way through, which says much for the ability of the merchant captains, for sailing in concert with other ships was totally alien to them. They would have prefered to take their chances alone, although the U-boats could outrun many of their tortoise-like commands, even when submerged.

With the fall of France in June 1940, the enemy's advantage increased, the new bases in the Bay of Biscay enabling even the small 500-ton coastal U-boats to operate up to 600 miles out in the Atlantic. Had Britain been able to gain the use of similar forward bases on the west coast of Ireland for her warships and aircraft, the odds would have been considerably shortened. But the Irish, although heavily subsidized by Britain and dependent on supplies carried across the Atlantic in British ships, stubbornly refused to violate their neutrality in Britain's favour. By the end of 1940, Britain and her few remaining allies had lost 1,281 merchant ships, totalling $4\frac{3}{4}$ million tons. This total had reached 7 million tons by June 1941, and there was worse to come.

The first Welsh ship to be sunk in the war was the Tatem Steam Navigation Company's *Winkleigh*, lost in the North Atlantic 5 days after the outbreak of hostilities. The last to go was also one of Tatem's, the 4,856-ton *Filleigh*, sunk off the North Foreland on 18 April 1945, within three weeks of the end of the war in Europe. In the intervening years, the ships of the Red Dragon were under constant and relentless attack. Slow, ungainly and usually heavily laden, they were easy meat for the U-boats and aircraft. In convoy, because of their characteristic lack of power, they were all too often unable to keep station, ending up as stragglers to be picked off at leisure by the shadowing U-boats. From 1940 onwards,

these ships were armed, but with ancient, unreliable 4-inch
and 12-pounder guns left over from another war. This armament was manned at first by the merchant seamen themselves,
who had undergone a three-day gunnery course, later gunners
of the Royal Navy and Maritime Anti-Aircraft Regiment, who
formed the DEMS (Defensive Equipment Merchant Ships)
force, took over. On the few occasions when they were able
to bring their guns into action, the Welsh ships gave a good
account of themselves but usually, caught by the unseen torpedo, they were on their way to the bottom before they could
retaliate.

As to the men themselves, the descendents of Prince Madoc
and John Lloyd, for many like Junior Engineer Oswald Frederick Swayne of Goodwick, the battle was mercifully short. For
others, it was a long, desperate struggle against impossible
odds, offering only the satisfaction of a job well done and culminating in the same lonely death without a grave. Captain Ebenezer Williams of Anglesey, gripped by a terrible premonition,
went down with the *Fiscus* in the North Atlantic on a cold
October night in 1940. Captain John Henry Reardon Smith
of Newport, his youngest son lost in the massacre of Convoy
HX 90, survived the sinking of the *Botavon* in 1942, only to
relinguish his command finally and irrevocably in the Indian
Ocean a year later. Captain Henry Thomas Isaac of Barry,
with the worst of the war behind him, died off Madagascar
in July 1943 in command of the same *Cornish City* which had
eluded the shells of the *Admiral Scheer* three years before when
under the command of Captain John O'Neill.

Those who died, and those who lived to see the peace, were
all quiet heroes, dedicated and uncomplaining. Yet, like all
British merchant seamen, they were to receive scant recogni-
tion for the indispensable part they played in saving their
country from extinction. They did not seek adulation but the
few civilian awards handed out – identical to those distributed
annually for diligent service in industry and commerce ashore
– were an insult to the men who had endured so much. It
was certainly not the pay and conditions that kept them coming

back to face the vicious onslaughts of the U-boats and the Focke-Wulfs voyage after voyage, year after year. At the best of times, the sea is a dangerous, comfortless job, demanding 10 to 12 hours a day, seven days a week, and understood only by those who endure it. In 1942, the pay of an Able Seaman was £12 a month, that of a Chief Officer around £27. On top of this came a 'War Risk Bonus' of £10 a month, which was really only a shamefaced attempt to prevent seamen's wages falling too far behind those ashore, many of whom, like the dockers and miners were regularly using strike action to further their own ends. To the men at sea, such conduct in war was incomprehensible and never to this day forgotten.

Out of a total Welsh fleet of 164 ships, no less than 123 were sunk. Inevitably the axe fell heaviest on the two largest companies, Sir William Reardon Smith and Evan Thomas, Radcliffe & Co. Of the 41 ships owned by Reardon Smith at the outbreak of the war, they were to lose 33, while Evan Thomas, Radcliffe & Co., lost 10 out of an original fleet of 24. Some of the smaller, but no less important, companies were annihilated, Tatem Steam Navigation losing 8 out of 8, Constants 7 of 7, Graig Shipping Company 4 out of 4, and so on down to the tiny Cardigan Shipping Company, which lost its only 2 ships. None of the Welsh shipping companies came through without a crushing loss in ships and men. The following chapters attempt to tell the story of some of those stalwart little ships and the gallant men who sailed them.

2

The Uskmouth: no phoney war at sea

At 11 o'clock on the morning of 3 September 1939, a sombre-voiced Prime Minister Neville Chamberlain informed the British people they were at war with Germany. For the second time in a generation the gates of Armageddon had been reached.

While the war on land and in the air was to take many months to break out into actual physical aggression, this was not the case at sea. Within ten hours of Chamberlain's epoch-making announcement, the German submarine *U-30*, commanded by Kapitän-Leutnant Fritz-Julius Lemp, sank without warning the 13,581-ton Donaldson passenger liner *Athenia*, which presented no more threat to the third Reich than did the women and children she was evacuating to the United States. The *Athenia* went down 250 miles to the northwest of Ireland with the loss of 112 passengers and crew. Lemp claimed to have mistaken the passenger ship for an armed merchant cruiser but his act was to set the pattern for a long and dirty war against British and Allied merchant shipping. By the third week in November the U-boats had sunk 66 British merchant ships, among them the Tatem Steam Navigation Company's *Winkleigh* and Reardon Smith's *Vancouver City*. The annihilation of the fleet of the Red Dragon had begun.

The convoy system, which had proved so successful in the First World War, was put into operation from the outset of the Second World War, with only fast vessels of the calibre of the *Athenia* taking the risks alone. Many merchant ship captains disliked the convoy system, seeing it as a dangerous bunching together of their mainly slow and cumbersome charges. This dislike was understandable, since no man who commands a commercially-orientated ship can ever find complete peace of mind when he is hemmed in on all sides. Searoom is his most sought-after asset. He is also accustomed to taking sole responsibility for the actions of his ship, being answerable to God and the Owner alone. To be forced to steam in company, at a regulated speed, on a course not of his choosing and subject to the discipline of Naval men often many years his junior in age and experience was, is, and always will be anathema to the captain of a merchant ship. But there are worse things in war than a temporary loss of independence. Few British masters refused to sail in a convoy in the Second World War but there were many who were denied its protection through no fault of their own.

In winter, to voyage from Sunderland to Monaco is to move from darkness into light. It is a journey from a cold, damp land plagued by industrial smog to a warm Elysium of clean air and sparkling blue water set against a background of mountains curtained with pristine snow. The distance by sea is a mere 2,000 miles but the passage is not without its perils. The fog-shrouded sandbanks of the North Sea, the crowded narrows of the English Channel and the ponderous swells of the Bay of Biscay must all be safely negotiated before the first welcoming kisses of a kinder climate are felt. Such was the prospect ahead for the crew of the steamer *Uskmouth* on a dreary day in November 1939.

The *Uskmouth*, built in 1928, was a small ship of only 2,483 tons gross and one of a fleet of three similar vessels owned by Richard W. Jones & Company of Newport Mon. Manned by a crew of twenty-five, she was a typical short-sea tramp of the coal trade of the 1930s. Her paintwork was faded by constant washing to remove the grime of her employment but she was, nevertheless, a personable little ship. In pre-war days, the ships of R. W. Jones had sported white-painted superstructures which, in an era when most tramps, especially colliers, favoured a serviceable brown or buff, must have been regarded as nothing short of ostentation. Certainly the white upperworks were a never-ending headache for the chief officers charged with the maintenance and cleanliness of these ships. As a concession to the war, now moving into its third month, the *Uskmouth*'s white paint had been covered by a drab grey but she still retained her stark black hull. It was as though the phlegmatic men who ran this ship regarded the war as a passing annoyance that would soon go away, allowing them to resume their old way of life. They were wrong.

The *Uskmouth* left Sunderland at 20.00 on the evening of 17 November loaded with 3,900 tons of coal for Monaco. She joined a coastal convoy, which would take her as far as Southend, in the Thames Estuary, where a larger convoy would form for the long, deep sea run down to the Straits of Gibraltar. As far as the *Uskmouth*'s master, Captain H. Hunter was concerned, his ship's presence in the coastal convoy had been a mistake from the start. He was indeed grateful for the protection offered by the Royal Navy but, despite the best efforts of the *Uskmouth*'s engineers, it was impossible for her to reach or maintain the speed of 9 knots specified by the convoy commodore. Limping along at 8½ knots, she had been a persistent straggler all the way down the North Sea. At the very least, a North Sea passage in winter is a harrowing exercise for the shipmaster. The visibility is invariably poor and the navigation marks few. For Captain Hunter, groping his way through the sandbanks paralleling the East Coast, and at the same time attempting to remain part of an organized body of ships half a knot faster than his maximum, the 30-hour passage was a nightmare he did not wish to repeat. Having eventually arrived off Southend Pier, he made his apologies to the convoy commodore and the *Uskmouth* set out for Gibraltar alone.

Forty-two hours later, the Welsh collier was clear of the constrictions of the English Channel and heading out into open water before turning southwest to cross the mouth of the Bay of Biscay. The weather was now fine, the visibility good and the long Atlantic swell muted. The heavily-laden ship had only a gentle, corkscrewing motion that would develop into a lazy roll when she turned beam-on to the swell. As she was sailing alone and unarmed, Hunter set his courses well clear of the land, first aiming for a point about 100 miles off Cape Finisterre, where he would then steam due south to the latitude of the Straits of Gibraltar. By remaining far out in the Atlantic for as long as possible, he hoped his ship would be safe from attack.

Given a functioning crystal ball, Hunter might well have decided to follow his old peacetime route, passing close in to Finisterre and hugging the Spanish and Portuguese coasts on his way south. He did not, however, possess such a clair-voyant aid and was not to know, therefore, that in his chosen path lay *U-43*, commanded by Kapitän-Leutnant Wilhelm Ambrosius. The U-boat had already been blooded earlier in the mouth by sinking two British ships, the *Arlington Court* and the *Pensilva*, within a few days of each other. Ambrosius was now waiting for his third victim.

Shortly before 23.00 on the night of the 25th, the *Uskmouth* was abeam, but out of sight of Cape Finisterre. A moderate swell was running, indicating a blow far out in the Atlantic, but the weather continued fine. Third Officer J. Robe, consol-ling himself that the last hour of his watch was near, was keeping a lonely vigil in the port wing of the bridge, sweeping the horizon from time to time with tired eyes. Suddenly he snapped alert. An ominous track of bubbles was streaking across from the port beam to the bow of the ship.

Robe threw himself into the wheelhouse, expecting at any moment to feel the shock of the explosion as the torpedo struck. Then, as his trembling fingers fumbled to remove the plug from the captain's voicepipe, he saw through the wheelhouse window that the line of bubbles had crossed the bow from port to starboard and was disappearing into the night. It had been a very near miss.

Captain Hunter was on the bridge within seconds of answer-ing the piercing whistle of the voicepipe. He was undecided whether the track the Third Officer had seen was that of a torpedo or the wash made by the U-boat's periscope as it cut across the *Uskmouth*'s bow. There was no indecision in his action, however.

Ordering the helm hard to starboard, Hunter swung the ship through an arc of 90 degrees, putting her stern on to his estimated position of the U-boat. At the *Uskmouth*'s speed of 8½ knots, there was little chance of running away, even from a submerged U-boat, but Hunter intended to present the most difficult target possible for his attacker.

Hardly had the collier settled on her course than Hunter glimpsed a phosphorescent track racing in from the starboard bow. This time there was no mistaking the wake of an approaching torpedo.

Deciding it was too late to alter course to avoid the torpedo, Hunter's next thought was for the safety of his crew, many of whom would be sleeping. Lunging for the lanyard of the steam whistle, he shattered his silence of the night with a succession of urgent blasts. As he did this, the torpedo passed close ahead, missing the *Uskmouth*'s bow by only a few feet.

In spite of the tense excitement on the bridge, Hunter now found time to instruct his wireless operator to transmit the signal SSS, followed by the *Uskmouth*'s position. This would warn all ships in the vicinity and the listening Admiralty that the vessel was being attached by a submarine. As this message was being tapped out, word was passed to the bridge that another torpedo had just crossed the stern from starboard to port. Repeating his earlier tactic, Hunter put the helm hard to port and again presented his ship's stern towards the estimated position of the unseen attacker.

Wilhelm Ambrosius, crouched at the periscope of *U-43*, was seething with frustration. Due to Hunter's tactics, what should have been a simple copybook sinking of a small, unarmed merchantman was becoming a most costly operation. *U-43* had already wasted three torpedoes, each carrying 360 kilos of high explosive and worth 40,000 Reichmarks apiece. Ambrosius decided it was time for the farce to end and gave the order to surface.

Hunter was in the act of steadying his ship on a southeasterly course, when he saw the U-boat surface on his port quarter at about 250 yards. Through his binoculars he saw men running along her casing towards the deck gun.

The shooting began almost at once, the first shells screaming between the *Uskmouth*'s masts to explode harmlessly in the sea on her starboard side. The U-boat's first intention was obviously to bring down the merchant ship's wireless aerials, thereby silencing her frantic calls for help. Hunter, without even a light machine gun to defend his ship, could do not more than order his crew to stand by the boats, while he did his best to spoil the U-boat's aim.

U-43's 88 mm gun's crew were either poor shots or they were severely handicapped by the darkness, for they completely failed to carry away the *Uskmouth*'s masts or aerials. When they tired of this thankless task, they lowered their sights and began the grim work of the night. Shell after shell smashed into the collier's superstructure, the range being so short that it was impossible for the U-boat's gunners to miss.

It became plain to Hunter, still on the bridge of the *Uskmouth*, the enemy was intent on destroying his ship with precious little regard for human life. Reluctantly, he swung the handle of the engineroom telegraph to stop and gave the order to abandon ship.

On receipt of the shouted order, the *Uskmouth*'s chief officer sprinted for the boat deck, where the rest of the crew, supervised by Third Officer Robe, were already swinging out the port lifeboat. Shells were bursting all around them and, although there was no panic, the men worked with feverish haste. Boatswain Dowie clambered into the boat, knocked away the gripes and the chief officer gave the order to lower away. At that moment, a shell exploded close by, sending a hail of shrapnel scything through the assembled men. Third Officer Robe and Able Seaman Davies were killed instantly and the forward fall of the lifeboat was severed. The bow of the boat plunged seawards, throwing Dowie into the dark water below.

Captain Hunter now arrived on the boat deck and, amid

the scream and crash of the shells, shepherded the dazed survivors towards the starboard boat, which was still intact. This boat was lowered without incident and the remaining 22 men of the *Uskmouth* piled aboard and cast off.

As there was still way on the ship, the lifeboat drifted rapidly astern, passing close to the U-boat, which was now pumping shells into the striken merchantman as fast as her gun's crew could fire. Standing in the stern of the lifeboat, Hunter watched helplessly as his ship was mercilessly pounded to pieces.

At 01.25 on the morning of 26 November, the *Uskmouth*, ablaze from stem to stern, gave a last shudder and slipped below the waves.

The actions of Wilhelm Ambrosius had been neither impressive nor humane. Faced with a small, slow and entirely unarmed merchant ship, he had, in direct contravention of the 1935 Geneva Convention, attempted to torpedo that ship without warning. Having failed miserably to do so, he had then surfaced and opened fire without giving the *Uskmouth*'s crew a reasonable chance to abandon ship. Only by a miracle and the disciplined behaviour of the merchant seamen, had very heavy casualties been avoided. As it was, three innocent men had died.

It may have been that Ambrosius felt his submarine threatened by the possible presence of British warships in the area – the convoy the *Uskmouth* had left off Southend was somewhere in the offing. More likely the German commander was so enranged by the frustration of his torpedo attack by Captain Hunter's evasive manouvering, that all his more humane feelings were momentarily stifled. In any event, it was a very hollow victory for Ambrosius, and one unlikely to bring praise from the C-in-C U-boats, Admiral Karl Dönitz. In addition to the three wasted torpedoes, *U-43* had expended nearly 100 rounds of 88 mm ammunition – and all to sink a 2,483-ton ship carrying nothing more vital than a few thousand tons of coal destined for a neutral country.

Having watched their ship sink and the U-boat slink into the darkness, Captain Hunter and the remaining 21 members of his crew hoisted the sails of their crowded lifeboat and set course for the Spanish coast, which Hunter estimated to be some 120 miles to the east. Fortunately, the weather held good and, for the rest of that night and throughout the next day, they sailed steadily towards the land.

At 23.00 on the 26th, having covered 110 miles, and when only five miles off Cape Villano, the lifeboat was sighted by the Italian steamer *Juventus* and Hunter and his men were picked up. Fortunately for the *Uskmouth*'s survivors, Italy had not yet entered the war and the *Juventus* was able to land them at Ramsgate four days later. They had spent only thirteen days at sea but in that short time had learned what they and their fellow merchant seamen would have to face time and time again over the following six years.

The *Uskmouth* fiasco was the turning point in the fortunes of *U-43*, for she then went on to sink over 100,000 tons of Allied shipping in the next three years or so. In one of her last actions of the war, when commanded by Oberleutnant Hans-Joachim Schwantke, she brought disgrace on herself by sinking the German blockade runner *Doggerbank*, which Schwantke had mistaken for a British ship. Five months later, on 30 July 1943, with no more sinkings to her credit, *U-43* was herself sunk by aircraft from the American carrier *Santee*, when 260 miles south-west of the Azores. Wilhelm Ambrosius, who moved out of active U-boat service in October 1940, and was later promoted to Fregatten-Kapitän, survived the war and died in Germany in September 1955.

3

The Llanarth: the 'happy time' begins

There were few signs of elation in Britain in June 1940. The bulk of the B.E.F. nearly 340,000 men, had been successfully evacuated from the beaches of Dunkirk but they had come home exhausted and without their arms. In war, defeat is defeat, no matter by which name you choose to call it. Italy had declared war on 10 June and, with the rest of Europe under subjugation and the United States of America deliberately turning its face away from the West, Britain was alone, except for the support of her dominions overseas. But vast and plenteous though these territories might be, the sea lanes joining them to the mother country were vunerable and increasingly threatened.

The evacuation of Dunkirk had cost the Royal Navy 25 destroyers either sunk or seriously damaged, and with Hitler's invasion barges now massing on the other side of the Channel, there were precious few escorts left over for convoy work. It was not uncommon to see 20 or 30 merchant ships escorted by a single armed tug, or a minesweeper, or with no protection other than the Admiralty's blessing. The month of June 1940 cost Britain's Merchant Navy 61 ships, totalling 282,560 tons.

For the U-boats, this was the beginning of the 'Happy Time', when men like Otto Kretschmer, Günther Prien and Engelbert Endrass were to reap a fearful harvest among the almost defenceless merchant ships of Britain and her Allies. Matching sinking for sinking with these seasoned aces was the young Fritz-Julius Lemp, who had already earned a place in history by sinking the *Athenia* in the opening days of the war.

Following the outcry over the sinking of the passenger ship,

s/s *Llanarth* 5053 GRT. Sunk in Western Approaches by *U-30* 28 June 1940.

Lemp was recalled to Germany for a severe reprimand but he was back in the North Atlantic by the end of December 1939 and in command of his old boat, *U-30*. By the third week in June 1940, Lemp was patrolling the south-western approaches to the British Isles, having added another 11 ships to his score, none of them passenger ships but all sunk without warning.

Since her maiden voyage in March 1929, the Evan Thomas, Radcliffe & Co. steamer *Llanarth* had been engaged on a 'triangular' trade, carrying coal from South Wales to the Mediterranean, then in ballast to South America and home again with grain. There was hard work in the trade for the *Llanarth*'s crew, with hatches to be cleaned after the discharge of the coal and shifting boards to be rigged for the grain – all on the ballast passage – but the round voyage was reasonably short and the weather good for much of the time. Inevitably, the war had put an end to this agreeable routine. Mid-June 1940 saw the 5,053-ton *Llanarth* in Freetown Sierra Leone, about to embark on the last leg of an 11,000 mile passage from Australia. Although the voyage had been long, much of it had been spent far away from the wearying tensions of the war. For the *Llanarth*'s 35-man crew, and especially for Captain John James Parry, the change had been welcome.

Sailing from Freetown on the 12th, the *Llanarth* set out unescorted for Falmouth, a distance of nearly 3,000 miles. She was riding low in the water, her hatches filled to capacity with 7,980 tons of flour, loaded at Melbourne. For much of the passage northwards, Captain Parry anticipated no problems, other than the normal, day to day worries of a shipmaster. His ship was slow but, for a merchantman of the day, well armed with, in addition to the usual machine guns, a 4-inch anti-submarine gun aft and a 12-pounder high/low angle gun on the forecastle head. However, anxious to minimize the risk to his vessel, Parry reached far out into the Atlantic, adhering strictly to the route given to him by the Naval Control in Freetown. As an added precaution, the *Llanarth* followed a timed zig-zag pattern of courses by day and in bright moonlight, in order to confuse any U-boat which might take to shadowing her. Only in complete darkness did she steer a straight course.

On the night of 27 June, having steamed 2,400 lonely miles without incident, the *Llanarth* was in the Western Approaches, some 250 miles to the south-west of Lands End. Being now in higher latitudes, darkness was slow to fall and it was 22.00 before Captain Parry deemed it safe to discontinue zig-zagging for the night. Having done this, he left the Third Officer in charge of the bridge and went below. He again visited the bridge at 23.00 and spent some time checking all was well. The night had taken on a deep, comforting blackness and it seemed, for the time being at least, the *Llanarth* was alone on an empty sea. However, she was now entering the English Channel and Parry remained on the bridge for another two hours before deciding it was safe for him to risk putting his feet up on his dayroom settee. He again went below.

Kapitän-Leutnant Lemp, in *U-30*, had reached the position BF 4192 on his German Naval grid system chart, which put him, in terms of latitude and longitude, in 47° 30′ N 10° 30′ W. He was well situated to monitor the approaches to both the St George's and English Channels. Sooner or later, he calculated, a convoy must come his way. But Lemp did not have to wait for a convoy, with its attendant dangers from escorting warships. Shortly after midnight, the low, square outline of a heavily laden merchant ship was seen on the dark horizon. After satisfying himself the merchant ship was alone, Lemp manouvered his boat into an advantageous position and, at two minutes past one on the morning of 28 June, gave order to fire.

Ideally, Lemp would have wished his torpedo to strike the merchant ship in her engineroom, thereby rendering her without power and flooding the largest single compartment of the ship. Unfortunately – or fortunately, depending on which side you should wish to favour – he had miscalculated. The 20-inch torpedo slammed into the *Llanarth*'s hull some fifty feet abaft the engineroom, in the region of her No. 5 hold. It exploded with a deafening roar.

Captain Parry, resting in his dayroom before facing the difficulties of the Channel passage, was thrown in the air by the force of the explosion. For a few moments, he lay dazed on the deck of his cabin, his nostrils filled with the acrid stench of burnt cordite. When his mind was able to grasp the awful fact that his ship had been torpedoed, he got to his feet and staggered across the room to the small safe against the bulkhead and hurriedly removed the ships confidential books and papers. These contained secret Admiralty codes, signals and pre-arranged routes, which Parry knew must not fall into enemy hands. Hurriedly stuffing the papers into the weighted canvas bag supplied for such an occasion as this, he stepped out on deck. The sight that greeted him there was more terrible than he had feared. The whole of the deck appeared to be in flames, the ship was listing to port and visibly beginning to settle by the stern. Without hesitation, Parry hurled the weighted bag into the sea. There would be no further need for Admiralty instructions now.

Taking the bridge ladder three steps at a time, Parry erupted into the wheelhouse, whose occupants, the Third Officer and the helmsman of the watch, were still in a state of shock. First giving the order to stop the *Llanarth*'s engine, Parry sent the helmsman aft to organize a fire party, its first priority to attempt to keep the flames away from the 4-inch magazine on the poop deck. Turning to the Third Officer, he ordered him to clear away the lifeboats. While there might still be a chance of saving the ship, Parry also considered it prudent to prepare for the worst.

After what seemed to Parry like hours, but was in reality only minutes, he was joined on the bridge by his Chief and Second Officers, both of whom had been off watch and asleep when the torpedo struck. The conference was brief and dramatic. Parry instructed the Second Officer to supervise the preparation of the lifeboats and then signalled the Chief Officer to follow him aft.

The scene on the after deck was chaotic and frightening

but perhaps not as hopeless as Parry had first thought. Tarpaulins, hatches and beams had gone from No. 5 hold, blown skywards by the explosion, and the cargo in the hold was well alight. Other fires had broken out on the poop deck amongst piles of dunnage wood stowed there and the 4-inch magazine was threatened, just as he had feared. The ship had a pronounced list to port but she did not yet appear to be in immediate danger of sinking. If the fires could be brought under control, there was still a chance of saving her. But as Parry and his Chief Officer set about organizing the fight, all steam pressure was lost in the engineroom and the *Llanarth*'s fire pumps ground to a halt, leaving the hoses limp and waterless in the hands of the fire party. Parry hurried over to the ship's side rail and looked down at the sea. It was now less than 3 feet from the deck. Sadly, he gave the order to lower the lifeboats.

Since shortly after being awoken by the explosion, the *Llanarth*'s wireless operator, following the pre-arranged emergency routine, had been unsuccessfully attempting to get away a distress message. It seemed likely the explosion had damaged his transmitter for, although he repeatedly tapped out his call for help on all possible frequencies, he received no reply. He reported his suspicions to Parry, who had called in the wireless room after leaving the blazing after deck. Parry asked him to keep trying until it was time to abandon ship. This the operator did, but without success, for no ship or shore station was to hear the *Llanarth*'s cries for help.

Both lifeboats were lowered and rowed clear of the ship's side without too much difficulty, although a heavy swell was running. Reluctant to leave his dying ship, and perhaps hoping for a miracle, Parry kept the two boats together and close to leeward of the *Llanarth*. By the light of the flames he examined the hull hoping to see the extent of the damage caused by the torpedo but whatever ghastly hole had been torn in his ship was now well below the waterline an unpluggable, gaping wound that would soon destroy her. After a while, mindful of the danger of exploding ammunition, Parry withdrew both boats to a safe distance and waited for the end.

The wind and sea were now rising and most of the occupants of the two boats were soon helpless with seasickness. After about twenty minutes, the flames on the *Llanarth* appeared to be dying down and Parry began to give thought to re-boarding. But it was only the waves quenching the fire as they washed over the slowly sinking ship. Some forty-five minutes after the *U-30*'s torpedo had struck, the *Llanarth* was gone.

Throughout the rest of the hours of darkness Parry attempted to keep the two lifeboats together but, with the weather deteriorating as a depression moved in from the Atlantic, he was unable to do so. When daylight came, just after 04.00 on this summer's morning, the Chief Officer's boat was nowhere in sight. Reluctant to lose touch with the rest of his crew, Parry put his own boat stern on to the waves, so as to make it ride more comfortably and set his men to rowing easily, barely keeping steerage way on the boat. A sharp lookout was kept for the other lifeboat and at about 08.00, with the sun climbing rapidly behind the gathering clouds, what appeared to be a dark sail was sighted on the horizon. Parry was at once tempted to row towards it but had second thoughts. The sail could also be the conning tower of a submarine and, without binoculars, he was unable to be sure. He decided not to take the risk of approaching. In the event, he probably made a wise decision for, in addition to *U-30*, three other U-boats attracted by reports of a convoy inward bound from the south, were also in the vicinity. Among them was *U-43*, killer of the unarmed *Uskmouth* seven months earlier.

During the following twenty-four hours, the weather worsened, the wind gradually working up to gale force. In their heaving cockleshell of a boat Parry and his men struggled to step the mast in order to hoist a sail which would have kept the boat running before the south westerly wind, and in the general direction of the land. The movement of the boat was so violent that this proved impossible and they were forced to continue rowing. By the morning of the 29th, every man in the boat was exhausted, his hands blistered and bleeding his back muscles on fire. Then, slowly the wind and sea began to drop and calling on their last reserves of strength, they were at last able to step the heavy mast and hoist sail.

All that day and for much of the night they sailed north-eastwards before a light wind but, a ship's lifeboat being cumbersome and having none of the sailing qualities of a yacht, their progress towards the land was painfully slow. At dawn on Sunday 30 June, they ran out of wind altogether and lay becalmed. There was little that Parry could do now except await the passage of events. He calculated the boat had moved far enough east to be in the path of ships bound in and out of the Irish Sea and the Channel and there was also the possibility of being sighted by patrolling British aircraft. If no rescue came, they would continue sailing towards the land when sufficient wind rose again. The passage of events proved far quicker than Parry had anticipated. Within an hour of the wind falling away, smoke was sighted on the horizon to the north. As the men in the boat watched, their spirits rising, the single wisp of smoke became two, then a dozen. Soon, a collection of masts and funnels began to rise above the horizon. Parry rallied his men and, once again, the oars dipped and the boat crept slowly through the water, its bows pointed hopefully towards the ships in the north.

Although the survivors bent their backs to the task, it soon became obvious, even to the most optimistic in the boat, that the convoy, which seemed to be on a north-easterly course, would pass too far off to sight their small boat. Desperation heightened by fear gave way to grim determination and the heavy oars dipped faster and faster. As, at last, they began to make perceivable progress through the water, their joy was compounded by the appearance of a Sunderland flying boat low over the water, heading in their direction. At first, the big flying boat failed to sight them and their cries of joy turned to curses. But the aircraft came back and circled over the lifeboat before flying off in the direction of the convoy. The oars were taken up with new enthusiasm and, as the convoy had now altered course – presumably on the next leg of its zig-zag pattern – the lifeboat and the columns of ships drew slowly together. Soon, an escort vessel was seen to break away from the convoy and head towards them with her bow wave creaming. Shortly before eight o'clock, the life boat was bumping alongside the Flower class corvette HMS *Gladiolus* and Parry and his men were climbing the scrambling nets to safety. But their ordeal was not yet over.

4

The Beignon: rescue ship

Of all the ships in Convoy SL 36 there was at least one most unsuited to be in its company. The 5,218-ton *Beignon*, owned by Morel Ltd. of Mountstuart Square, Cardiff, built in 1939, was outwardly a conventional 5-hatch cargo ship of her day but her engineroom housed a powerful diesel engine built by William Doxford of Sunderland, Britain's experts in the marine diesel field. This engine gave the *Beignon* a top speed of 12 knots, a good 3 knots faster than most of the coal-fired steamers making up the convoy, which was to make the passage to the UK at the dignified, but highly vunerable speed of $7\frac{1}{2}$ knots. In hindsight, it seems clear that, had the *Beignon* used her superior speed to sail independently, she might well have lived to meet a quiet, if ignominious, end in a shipbreaker's yard some thirty years later. As it turned out, her presence in Convoy SL 36 drew her into a tangled web of coincidence and destruction, which ended in tragedy on a fine summer's morning in July 1940.

Convoy SL 36 left the busy anchorage of Freetown harbour at 13.00 on 16 June. Steaming in line astern, the ships passed close to the tall lighthouse on Cape Sierra Leone, pulled well clear of the dangers of Carpenter Rock and formed up in orderly columns for the long passage north. The convoy was in two sections, ships bound for Liverpool, Glasgow and the Bristol Channel being on the port wing, while those in the starboard wing were heading for London and East Coast ports. The Naval commodore controlling the convoy was in the 13,376-ton Blue Star ship *Avelona Star*. Protection was provided by HMS *Dunvegan Castle*, an Armed Merchant Cruiser of 15,007 tons. The *Beignon*, at the time of sailing uncertain of her port of discharge, was in the port wing of the convoy at position No. 13, a numerical position which must have given rise to some sour faces on board the Welsh ship.

The convoy's northward route lay between the bulge of Africa and the Cape Verde Islands, thence west of the Canaries, east of the Azores and then in a long curve towards the western approaches to the British Isles. Although deep laden under 8,816 tons of wheat, the *Beignon* had no difficulty in keeping station as the convoy zig-zagged northwards through the tropics. Her master, Captain W. J. Croome had confidence in his ship, her crew and the 12-pounder and 4-inch guns she was armed with. The weather was fine and was expected to remain so, at least until the Western Approaches were reached. Then, the unpredictable British maritime climate would take over, bringing with it, even in these months of high summer, anything from dense fog to a howling gale. Croome was content to cross these bridges when he came to them.

In the early hours of the morning of 28 June, when Convoy SL 36 was roughly abeam of Lisbon, 550 miles to the north the *Llanarth* was on fire and sinking after being torpedoed by *U-30*. No word of this attack reached the convoy, which was now unwittingly sailing into a trap being carefully set up by Admiral Dönitz, Befehlshaber der Unterseeboote (Cin C Submarines). Lemp, with the stench of the burning *Llanarth* still in his nostrils, was to be joined by Korvetten-Kapitän Hans-Gerrit von Stockhausen in *U-65*, Kapitän-Leutnant Heinz Scheringer in *U-26* and Kapitän-Leutnant Wilhelm Ambrosius in *U-43*, who had despatched the unfortunate *Uskmouth* in the previous September. The first of the wolf-packs was gathering.

For the sheep of Convoy SL 36, the greater part of their 3,000 mile trek northwards was accomplished without incident and by the 30th they were crossing the Bay of Biscay with a growing air of confidence. Their sole escort, HMS *Dunvegan Castle*, had been joined by destroyers and corvettes of Western

Command, while Sunderlands of Coastal Command kept a watchful eye on the convoy from time to time. That morning, as breakfast was being passed up from the galleys, those on deck were witness to the rescue of the *Llanarth*'s survivors by HMS *Gladiolus*. It was a heartening sight but had a bad omen for the coming day.

At three minutes past noon, von Stockhausen in *U-65* opened up the score for the wolf-pack by torpedoing the 5,802-ton cargo liner *Clan Ogilvy*. The fragile peace of the day was abruptly shattered by the thunder of exploding depth charges as the escorts raced into action. Their prompt retaliation prevented von Stockhausen from administering the coup de grace to the *Clan Ogilvy*, which although damaged forward, was still afloat. The other U-boats also held back and the convoy, now fully alerted, proceeded warily on its way.

Late the same afternoon, when about 200 miles to the northwest of Cape Finisterre, Captain Croome received orders to take the *Beignon* to Newcastle to discharge her cargo of wheat. As a result of these orders, the convoy commodore directed the *Beignon* to change her position to the starboard wing of the convoy joining those ships already bound for the East Coast. This manoeuvre, which involved pulling out of the ranks and steaming around astern of the convoy to take up a position at the rear of the outer column of the starboard wing, was completed by 18.00. When the night began to close in, the commodore who was in the Blue Star liner *Avelona Star*, ordered the *Beignon* to act as rescue ship in the event of a night attack by the U-boats. As a 'tail-ender' capable of a good turn of speed, the *Beignon* was eminently suited for this work.

The Welsh ship was called upon to act out her new role far sooner than expected and, ironically, her first customer was the commodore's own ship.

At 21.15, Croome saw the *Avelona Star*, which was about one mile ahead of the *Beignon*, erupt in a cloud of smoke and steam. Wilhelm Ambrosius in *U-43* had fired the first shot of the night.

When the smoke from the explosion cleared away, the

13,376-ton meat carrier could be seen listing to starboard and settling slowly in the water. While the rest of the convoy dispersed and the escorts went into their defensive routine, Croome brought the *Beignon* round and raced for the crippled ship. For the next two hours, although under constant threat of being torpedoed, he kept his ship close in to the sinking *Avelona Star*, picking up 83 of her 85-man crew. The remaining two men were rescued by the *Dunvegan Castle*.

As passengers in HMS *Gladiolus*, Captain John James Parry and his men were reluctant witnesses to the attack on Convoy SL 36. They were to see three merchant ships sunk before *Gladiolus* left the convoy with the object of landing the *Llanarth*'s survivors at Plymouth. The corvette had not pulled ahead of the other ships more than two miles when *U-26* put a torpedo into the United Africa Company's 4,871-ton *Zarian*. The *Gladiolus* immediately reversed course and joined in the search for the U-boat. Luck was not with Heinz Scheringer that night. The *Zarian* remained afloat and the full fury of the escorts was let loose on *U-26*. She was eventually sunk by HMS *Rochester*, Scheringer and his crew being taken prisoner.

After playing her part in the attack on *U-26*, *Gladiolus* was detailed to stand by the damaged *Zarion* for the night and the next morning was given the task of escorting *Clan Ogilvy* which, with her bow blown off, was attempting to make port stern first. Parry and his men were to spend another forty-eight hours on the crowded corvette before being landed at Plymouth on the morning of 3 July. There Parry received the good news that the rest of his men, in the *Llanarth*'s second lifeboat, had also been rescued.

The *Beignon* had been left far behind the convoy as she worked assiduously to rescue the crew of the *Avelona Star*. As soon as this was complete, at 22.15 on the 30th, Croome, acutely conscious of the vunerability of his ship, made all speed in an effort to catch up with SL 36. As a precaution against surprise attack, he used an unorthodox zig-zag pattern and kept his guns continuously manned with the help of spare gunners from the *Avelona Star*'s crew. Thus prepared, he pushed on through the night, hopeful of rejoining the convoy soon after daylight on the 1st. He was unaware that *U-30* was shadowing the convoy.

Dawn came early on the 1st day of July, the sky to the eastwards beginning to lighten shortly after 03.30. The promise of a warm sun rising on a fine day breathed new life into the 4-inch gun's crew standing-to on the *Beignon*'s poop. The unspoken fears of the night slipped quickly away and the men looked forward with confidence to reaching the safety of the convoy's escort screen within a few hours.

Daylight brought no such comfort to Kapitän-Leutnant Lemp who, in *U-30*, had spent the night on the suface shadowing SL 36. Mindful of the threat posed by patrolling aircraft, Lemp was forced to take his boat below the waves as soon as the sky began to pale. With her speed reduced to a crawl and her battery power draining away with every hour that passed, *U-30* was unlikely to increase her score that day. Lemp could scarcely believe his good fortune when he saw the merchant ship coming up astern with a bone in her teeth. At 03.45, a torpedo tracked across the *Beignon*'s stern from port to starboard, rudely jerking the 4-inch gun's crew out of their early morning reverie. The gunlayer dived for the bridge telephone. Twenty minutes later, Croome, who had reached the bridge shortly after the telephoned warning from the poop, saw a second torpedo narrowly miss his ship. The short hairs on the back of his neck began to rise, for he knew it was only a matter of time before his unseen attacker found the correct deflection.

The third torpedo followed close on the heels of the second and was not seen from the bridge. There was a violent explosion that seemed to Croome to lift the *Beignon* bodily into the air and stop her dead in her tracks. She appeared to have been hit on the starboard side about 150 feet from the bow. The ship began to settle quickly by the head and it was at once obvious to Croome that she had little time left. It was unnecessary for him to give the order to abandon ship, for his crew and the survivors of the *Avelona Star*, alerted following the opening of the attack thirty minutes earlier, were already lowering the boats and launching the liferafts. With a total of 116 men to evacuate, time was of the essence. Croome stayed on the bridge until all the boats and rafts were clear, then went below to search the accommodation. Having satisfied himself that no one else remained on board, he slipped on his life jacket and returned to the bridge, determined not to leave his ship until all hope of saving her was gone.

Croome did not have long to wait. At 04.23, eight minutes after *U-30*'s torpedo had struck, the *Beignon* dipped her savaged bow under the swell for the last time and sank. Croome, still on the bridge, was taken down with her.

After what seemed an eternity, Croome was able to break free of the suction created by his dying ship and kicked his way to the surface. Fortunately the sea was calm and, within a few minutes, he found himself clinging to a floating spar, in company with one of his young apprentices. With his head only a few inches above the water, he was unable to sight any of the *Beignon*'s lifeboats or rafts and he realized at once that the hopes of rescue for himself and his young companion were very slim. The *Beignon* had been some thirteen miles astern of the convoy and out of sight when she was hit and it was unlikely the explosion would have been heard by the other ships. Worse still, her wireless transmitter had been damaged and no SOS had been sent. The likelihood of a search being organized for survivors of a ship which was probably not yet known to be sunk was very remote indeed.

The two men were saved by the impetuousity of Korvetten-Kapitän Hans-Gerrit von Stockhausen who, in *U-65* had made the mistake of torpedoing the *Clan Ogilvy* in daylight on the previous day. Almost two hours after the *Beignon* went down, the escorts HMS *Vesper* and HMS *Gladiolus*, who had been standing by the damaged Clan liner during the night, came up at full speed, anxious to rejoin the convoy. Keen-eyed lookouts spotted Croome and the apprentice in the water and they were soon safe on board HMS *Vesper*. Thirty-six hours later, they were landed at Plymouth to join company with the

Llanarth's survivors, brought in by the *Gladiolus*. Of the rest of the *Beignon*'s crew, two were lost and one died after rescue. Five men of the *Avelona Star* also lost their lives in the torpedoing of the Welsh ship.

To *U-30*, the reckoning for the sinking of the *Llanarth* and the *Beignon* came later that year, when she was damaged and abandoned by her crew. Swift action by a Royal Naval boarding party secured the U-boat before she could sink. Fritz-Julius Lemp was not in command at the time. he was to die in *U-110*, while attacking Convoy OB 318 in the North Atlantic on 9 May 1941. Forced to the surface by depth charges dropped by the corvette *Aubrietia*, *U-110* was then fired on by destroyers *Broadway* and *Bulldog* and eventually boarded and captured, only to sink eleven hours later. *Aubrietia* picked up survivors from *U-110*. Fritz-Julius Lemp was not among them.

5

The King City: Indian Ocean raider

In February 1941, British land forces, pushing north from the Kenyan border, advanced into Italian Somaliland, sweeping all before them. The Italians, having little stomach for the fight, disappeared into the barren hinterlands of Ethiopia, leaving behind them the vast quantities of stores, arms and ammunition. In their hurry to depart, Mussolini's disillusioned men also abandoned a prisoner of war camp of which they had good reason to be ashamed. When British troops entered this camp, sixty miles to the north of Mogadishu, they found 194 British merchant seamen living in the depths of privation and degradation. Dirty, half-starved, wracked by dysentery, and with their clothes in tatters, the men were survivors of merchant ships sunk by the German raider *Atlantis*. Thirty-eight of them were survivors of the Reardon Smith vessel *King City*, which had gone down under the guns of the *Atlantis* more than six months earlier.

The idea of using armed merchant ships to attack the enemy's merchant shipping was born in the First World War, when German's Imperial Navy was securely bottled up in its own ports by the Royal Navy. On 21 December 1916, the German windjammer *Seeadler*, commanded by Graf Felix von Luckner, slipped past the British blockade of the North Sea disguised as the Norwegian barque *Hero*, bound for Australia. Concealed beneath her deck cargo of timber were two 4.2-inch guns and below her after deck planking was a powerful auxiliary engine. By the time she was shipwrecked in the Society Islands seven months later, the *Seeadler* had sailed 30,000 miles and accounted for 14 Allied merchant ships worth in the region of £6 million. The surface raider had arrived.

The *Atlantis*, commanded by Kapitän-zur-See Bernhard Rogge, bore no resemblance to the *Seeadler*, yet she was her direct descendant. Built in 1923 for the Hansa Line of Bremen as the *Goldenfels*, she was of 7,862 tons gross, with a top speed of 18 knots. Commandeered by the German Navy in 1939, she was put into Kiel, where she was equipped with six 5.9-inch guns, 4 torpedo tubes, light and heavy machine guns, 93 mines and 2 Arado seaplanes. All this panoply of war was hidden away behind portable screens or below decks so that the *Atlantis* retained the innocent appearance of her former days as a cargo liner. Although her 5.9's were forty years old, she was in reality a most formidible raider, all the more dangerous for her ability to pose as an innocent neutral merchant-man. Manned by 347 naval personnel, she set sail from Kiel on 31 March 1940, her aim to create the maximum possible havoc amongst Allied shipping in the Indian Ocean.

Six weeks later, the 4,744-ton *King City*, taken into service as a collier by the Royal Navy, left Cardiff with 5,000 tons of coal, bound for Singapore via the Cape of Good Hope.

No seaman worthy of the name will ever admit to more than a mere touch of sadness when he quits his home port on a long voyage. To do so would undermine that inner determination that, voyage after voyage, sustains him in the swift transformation from life ashore to life at sea; to move from the relaxed atmosphere of home and loved ones into the regulated, isolated world of a ship. In times of war, with the everyday dangers of seagoing increased one hundredfold, the crossing of the line is even more difficult.

The *King City*'s four apprentices were young enough not to be troubled by such mundane problems when their ship left Cardiff in mid-July 1940. Leslie Bayley, Alexander Davidson, Aubrey Radford and Leslie Thomas were all, give or take a month or two, seventeen years old, fresh-faced, open-minded and filled with enthusiasm for the voyage ahead. Wonderful new worlds were waiting over the horizon. For Captain Harry Marshall, commanding the twelve year old *King City*, the forthcoming voyage held no such delights. Ahead of him lay a run of 11,700 miles; at least 46 days at sea, during which, unescorted for much of the time, his ship would be constantly exposed to danger. His current information was that the U-boats were now sinking 14 British ships a week, their sphere of action extending south to Sierra Leone, and beyond. It seemed quite likely some of the U-boats, attended by supply ships, would soon be operating off the Cape of Good Hope, where the pickings would be rich. As for the Indian Ocean, which the *King City* would have to cross alone, there was strong talk of one, perhaps two, German surface raiders at large. These would pose a very real threat, against which the *King City* could only muster an ancient 4-inch gun mounted on her poop.

Contrary to Captain Marshall's fears the *King City* traversed the Atlantic from north to south without molestation. Rounding the Cape of Good Hope in the first week of August, Marshall set course to pass well to the south of the approaches to the Mozambique Channel. It was quite obvious to him that this channel, which separates Madagascar from the African mainland and is traditionally the route used by ships bound to and from India and the Suez, would be closely watched by German raiders and the U-boats abroad in the Indian Ocean. Marshall did not breathe easily until he had passed the island of Mauritius and had settled the *King City* on the long north-westerly leg across the lonely waters of the Indian Ocean towards the Malacca Straights, gateway to Singapore.

Since leaving German waters at the end of March, the *Atlantis* had already more than justified the confidence placed in her by the Kriegsmarine. On her way south she had fallen in with and sunk the British merchant ship *Scientist* off Angola on 3 May and had successfully laid her deadly cargo of mines off Cape Aghulas on the 18th. The portents for her continued success were good. During the next three months, moving deeper into the Indian Ocean all the time, she sank four more Allied merchant ships, each one despatched quickly and cleanly without damage to herself.

Late on the night of 24 August the *Atlantis* was idling some 180 miles to the northeast of Rodriguez Island, a tiny tropical paradise lying 800 miles to the east of Madagascar. The weather was anything but paradisiacal, for the southern winter was not yet done and the wind was high, the sea rough and the sky heavily overcast, with a thin, miserable drizzle falling. The *Atlantis* was very close to the other ship before her lookouts sighted her.

Called to the bridge, Rogge examined the dark outline of the ship through his binoculars. She had the appearance of an Allied merchantman but she was acting in a most unorthodox manner. Far from making maximum speed and perhaps zig-zagging, as an unescorted merchant ship would be expected to do in these waters, she was steaming at slow speed and stopping from time to time. Mindful of the fact that several British armed merchant cruisers were reported to be in the area, Rogge was suspicious. He turned the *Atlantis* and steamed parallel to the unknown ship, matching her slow speed. The longer he observed her actions, the more he became convinced she was a British AMC and, as such, posed a deadly threat to his ship.

It is an established fact that, in the small hours, the human mind is at its lowest ebb and liable to magnify the unexplained out of all proportion. It is possible that for this reason it did not occur to Rogge that, had the other ship been a British AMC, her lookouts would have been every bit as alert as his own, and either a challenge or a broadside would have come his way long since. In the event, the *Atlantis* continued to shadow her suspected adversary, waiting for the dawn.

Aboard the *King City*, it had been one of those nights sent to try the patience of even the most equable of seamen. The miserable weather had coincided with the breakdown of one of the boiler room fans, without which the ship could not raise sufficient steam to keep the engines turning. A night-long battle fought by her engineers had kept the *King City* limping through the stormy darkness at a reduced speed, stopping and drifting from time to time as each attempted repair came to naught. As dawn began to push back the shadows of the wheelhouse, the *King City*'s Chief Officer became aware of the silent, ominous outline of a ship apparently shadowing them. He reached for the signal lamp, intending to challenge.

At that moment Kapitan-zur-See Rogge decided he was almost certainly confronted by a British armed merchant cruiser which presented a serious threat to his own ship. At his signal, the *Atlantis* ran up her battle ensigns and opened fire with her 5.9-inch guns. The range was so short it was impossible for the experienced German naval gunners to miss the almost stationary merchant ship. The first two shells exploded in the *King City*'s midships accommodation, killing instantly her four apprentices, her assistant cook and her deck boy, who still lay in their bunks in the innocence of sleep. Not one of them would ever see his eighteenth birthday.

Within minutes of being hit, the *King City* was ablaze from end to end, the gas generated by the 5,000 tons of coal in her holds turning her into a gigantic, self-feeding inferno. It was very much to Bernhard Rogge's credit that, as soon as he realized he had fired on a harmless cargo ship without warning, his first thought was to save what lives he could. The sea was rough and the swell running high and no real blame could have been attached to Rogge if he had left the men of the *King City* to their fate. But the German captain was a humane man. He ordered his First lieutenant, Ulrich Mohr, to take the boats away. Approaching the burning ship, Mohr was able to confirm Rogge's conclusions beyond doubt. She was a far cry from an armed merchant cruiser, her only armament being an old 4-inch gun on her poop, which was unmanned, its barrel pointing pathetically at the blood-red sky. In no sense could this ship have presented a threat to the *Atlantis*. But the damage had been done.

As the two whalers came within 300 yards of the *King City*, the fierce heat of the flames could be felt and Mohr saw men on the deck of the doomed ship struggling desperately to lower lifeboats and rafts. A number of men had already jumped into the water to escape the uncontrollable blaze. Despite the heavy seas, Mohr brought his boats alongside the *King City* and was able to effect the rescue of all 38 survivors, including some wounded, whom Captain Marshall refused to leave behind.

Although alight from bow to stern like a great, elongated gas torch, the *King City* brought credit to her British builders by stubbornly refusing to sink. Eventually, an impatient Rogge was forced to close range and expend more ammunition on the flaming wreck. When she did finally slip beneath the waves, the ship did so with an angry hissing of steam as the sea came into contact with her red hot superstructure. Once safe aboard the *Atlantis*, the *King City*'s survivors expressed their gratitude to Rogge and Mohr for their rescue but they were, at the same time, bitter at what they saw as the unnecessary killing of their six young men. It was as though the whole youth of their small, ship-bound community had been wiped out for no good reason other than a suspicion that their ship was hostile. The men of the *Atlantis*, Rogge in particular, would have it otherwise. They genuinely regretted the deaths of the young men, but argued, understandably, that they could not afford to take chances. For the *Atlantis* one mistake might be one too many.

By the middle of October, with another string of merchant ships to her credit, the *Atlantis* began to run into serious problems. In addition to her 347 crew, she now had on board over 300 prisoners. Food and water were becoming short and the accommodation available for the prisoners was dangerously over-crowded. However, salvation came on the 22nd, when the raider captured the Yugoslav tramp *Durmitor* in the Sunda Straight. The 5,000 ton, 28 year-old *Durmitor* – in her better days the British ship *Plutarch* – was a seedy, run-down ship, rusty, dirty and loaded with a full cargo of bulk salt. To Rogge she was a means to an end. With an armed prize crew aboard her and 240 ex-*Atlantis* prisoners penned in a barred wire compound on her deck, the *Durmitor* set sail for the nearest Axis-held port, Mogadishu in Italian Somaliland.

It was to be a voyage of misery for the prisoners, who

included Captain Harry Marshall and his 37 survivors from the *King City*. At night and in bad weather, the only shelter the prisoners had was in the *Durmitor*'s No. 1 and 2 holds, on top of the cargo of bulk salt. Here it was always cold, damp and overrun with giant rats, of which the Yugoslav carried a veritable army. To add to this came hunger and thirst. The 3,400-mile passage across the Indian Ocean to Mogadishu should have taken the *Durmitor* about nineteen days at her average speed of $7\frac{1}{2}$ knots but her Yugoslav chief engineer, to cover up some previous malpractice, had produced a ficticious set of bunker figures. The ship did not, in fact have anything like enough coal to reach Mogadishu. Speed was reduced to conserve fuel, so that the estimated nineteen days became twenty-nine and the prisoners suffered the additional privations of food and water rationing.

The *Durmitor*, having burned most of her cabin furniture and hatchboards in her boiler furnaces, finally fetched up near the small village of Uarsiech, forty miles to the north of Mogadishu, on 20 November. The prisoners, many of them now in a very sorry state, were put into an Italian prisoner of war camp, where conditions were to prove, if anything, worse than they were on the *Durmitor*. Here they remained for four long months, during which time four men died of dysentery and fever was rampant throughout the camp.

When the men of the *King City* – all fortunately still alive – and their fellow prisoners were released from captivity by the Gold Coast Regiment in March 1941, they were sick, emaciated and mentally drained. Yet, while they had harsh things to say about their treatment in the hands of the Germans and Italians, they were bitterly disappointed and hurt at their reception by the British authorities in Somaliland. While there seemed to be an excellent standard procedure for dealing with ex-prisoners from the Armed Forces, the merchant seamen were treated like lepers and left to fend for themselves. It was a bitter pill for men to swallow who had lost their ships and suffered months of hardship and captivity for their country.

Nine months after the survivors of the *King City* were set

free, luck finally ran out for the *Atlantis*. On the morning of 21 November, while she was stopped to the north of Kerguelen Island re-fuelling *U-126*, she was spotted by a Walrus from the cruiser HMS *Devonshire*, which was patrolling the area. *Devonshire* came racing in and the raider was soon under fire. A shell hit her magazine and she blew up and sank, taking seven of her men with her. The *Atlantis* which, in her short piratical career, sank 22 merchant ships totalling 135,697 tons, was no more.

The story did not end there for the survivors of the *Atlantis*. Concerned about the presence of *U-126* which had quickly submerged at the start of the attack, Captain R. D. Oliver, commanding *Devonshire*, withdrew from the scene without picking up survivors from the sunken raider. *U-126*, commanded by Kapitän-Leutnant Ernst Bauer, then surfaced and took the boats of the *Atlantis* in tow, handing them over two days later to the German supply ship *Python*. They were still on board that ship when, on 1 December, she stopped to refuel the submarines *U-A* and *U-68*. Over the horizon on this occasion came *Devonshire*'s twin sister HMS *Dorsetshire*. For the second time the men of the *Atlantis* found themselves taking to the boats from a ship on fire and sinking. Thereafter followed an amazing rescue operation carried out by four U-boats, who crammed the 400 survivors into their hulls and transported them safely back to Germany. Ulrich Mohr enjoyed the hospitality of the Italian submarine *Tazzoli*, commanded by Carlo Fecia di Cossato, who has another role to play in this book.

6

The Beatus and the Fiscus: north Atlantic massacre

The Canadian port of Three Rivers lies on the St Maurice River near to the point where it empties into the St Lawrence Estuary, almost 800 miles from the sea. In the war years, Three Rivers was one of the main loading terminals for the vast quantities of steel and timber flowing from Canada across the Atlantic to a beleaguered Britain. In late September 1940, two of the berths in the port were occupied by the steamers *Beatus* and *Fiscus*, comprising fifty per cent of the Tempus Shipping Company's fleet.

The Cardiff shipping company of Sir William Seager, otherwise Tempus Shipping, owned only four ships at the outbreak of the war. They were the usual run-of-the-mill South Wales tramps, distinguished only by their unusual names, *Amicus*, *Beatus*, *Fiscus* and *Salvus*. They were, however, known worldwise as being among the most efficient and best kept ships sailing out of South Wales. The *Salvus* had already received her baptism of fire in the North Sea, when she had successfully fought off an attack by German bombers earlier in the year. Her three sisters had so far eluded the enemy which, thirteen months into a war that had to date claimed nearly 500 British merchant ships, must have been some considerable satisfaction to Sir William Seager and his men. This equable state of affairs was unfortunately about to be upset.

The *Beatus*, of 4,885 tons, commanded by Captain William Brett and the *Fiscus* also of 4,885 tons, under Captain Ebenezer Williams, lay close together in Three Rivers, forming a tiny enclave of Wales in this vast, tree-covered New World. Neither ship was in the first bloom of her youth, the *Beatus* being built in 1925, while the *Fiscus* was only five years her junior. However, in the tradition of Tempus Shipping, both ships were in first class condition and, in more normal times, would have been well fitted for the coming voyage across the North Atlantic.

Captain Brett of the *Beatus* was in good spirits as the loading of his ship neared completion. His cargo was a satisfying one, being full cubic and full deadweight, a state of loading rarely achieved. At the bottom of the lower holds of the *Beatus* was stowed a layer of heavy steel ingots, with the remaining space right up to the hatch-tops packed with planks of Canadian timber. On deck, to a height of 12 feet, was stowed more timber. Not one cubic inch of space nor one inch of freeboard had been wasted. It was also of comfort to Brett that, should his ship take a torpedo, her cargo of timber would keep her afloat for a considerable time. In the North Atlantic, that could mean all the difference between life and death for Brett and his crew.

On board the *Fiscus*, Captain Ebenezer Williams was in a less happy frame of mind. The planners had seen fit to load his ship with a full deadweight cargo of steel ingots, topped off with a few crates of aircraft. In consequence, the *Fiscus* had too much weight too low down in her holds and was therefore guaranteed to roll her scuppers under all the way across the Atlantic. A torpedo would send her to the bottom like a stone. It was this last possibility that weighed heavily Williams's mind. He had survived the first World War at sea and, so far, this one, but he had a strong premonition that the final reckoning would come soon. In his dour, North Walian way he had made known his fears to Brett, who had done his best to dispel them, but Ebenezer Williams would have none of it. He was convinced neither he nor the *Fiscus* would see the other side of the Atlantic.

The two Welsh ships duly joined Convoy SC 7 on 4 October at Sydney, Cape Breton, at the entrance to the Gulf of St Lawrence. It is doubtful if Brett and Williams took any heart at the sight of the 33 elderly ships they found assembled in the large and sheltered bay of Sydney harbour. The Commodore of the convoy was in residence in the twenty-six-year old *Assyrian*, a cargo vessel of less than 3,000 tons, which would have been more at home in the Mediterranean than in the North Atlantic at the equinox. Someone – and experienced seaman he cannot have been – had also decided to send with this convoy the Great Lakes steamers *Eaglescliffe Hall*, *Trevisa* and *Winona*, each of only 1,800 tons gross and well past pensionable age. Here also was Sir William Reardon Smith's *Botusk*, herself twenty-one years old and only a little over 3,000 tons. The others, half of them under the Red Ensign, could only be described as a motley collection of rusty geriatrics, all about to set sail into a hostile ocean dominated by the enemy.

The 35 ships of SC 7 set out from Sydney on 5 October, led by the diminutive *Assyrian* and escorted by the Canadian armed yacht *Elk* and the 1,000-ton sloop HMS *Scarborough*. It was hardly an assembly to strike fear into the enemy's heart or, for that matter, to boost the confidence of those involved. On the credit side, the weather was good, fine and clear with no more than a fresh breeze blowing. However, the North Atlantic seldom rests easy for long and the winter gales soon came sweeping in. On the 7th HMCS *Elk*, short of fuel and unable to withstand the seas, turned back, leaving *Scarborough* as the sole escort. Four other ships, including the 1,800-ton *Trevisa*, also fell out and were left to straggle along behind.

Fighting to hold ranks, the remainder of the convoy pushed slowly westwards, challenging the worsening weather for every mile gained. By the 16th, at the northern-most point of their route and still unmolested by the enemy, hopes were running high. They were only four days steaming from the Northern Approaches and the hard-pressed *Scarborough* had been joined by the sloop HMS *Fowey* and the corvette HMS *Bluebell*. It was then they heard the plaintive calls for help from the little *Trevisa*, straggling astern. The U-boats had made their first kill. The ships moved closer together and waited for the coming onslaught. As if sensing the approaching drama, the wind fell and the sea ceased its angry raging.

SC 7 did not have long to wait. At just before midnight on the 16th, Kapitän-Leutnant Heinrich Bleichrodt in *U-48*, who had been aimlessly scanning an empty ocean with his binoculars, sighted the slow-moving mass of ships. Bleichrodt immediately radioed Lorient for assistance and began to stalk his prey.

On receipt of Bleichrodt's sighting report, Admiral Dönitz ordered his North Atlantic force into action. In the area were Otto Kretschmer in *U-99*, Engelbert Endrass in *U-46*, Fritz Frauenheim in *U-101*, Joachim Schepke in *U-100* and Karl-Heinz Moehle in *U-123*. Between them these ace commanders had already accounted for a total of 78 Allied merchant ships. Now they raced to station themselves in a north-south line ahead of the convoy, a lethal trap into which SC 7 must sail.

At 05.00 on the 17th, Heinrich Bleichrodt began his lone attack with a fan of torpedoes which sank the 3,843-ton *Scoresby*, the French tanker *Languedoc* and damaged the 4,678-ton *Haspenden*. But, in attacking on the surface and so near to dawn, Bleichrodt had made a mistake that proved almost fatal for *U-48*. A Sunderland flying boat of Coastal Command, the first air cover for the convoy, spotted the marauding submarine and dived to the attack. The Sunderland's bombs did no damage to *U-48* but Bleichrodt was forced to go deep. If *U-48* had then been ignored, for she had suffered a severe shock and was unlikely to return to the attack, the tragedy that befell SC 7 in the next 72 hours might have been lessened. Unfortunately, *Scarborough* gave chase, spending most of the day hunting *U-48*. By the time the sloop broke off empty-handed, she was so far astern of the convoy that she was never able to rejoin.

In the early hours of the 18th, SC 7 had acquired a new shadower, in the form of *U-38*, commanded by Heinrich Liebe, who had also come upon the ships by chance. After reporting the convoy's position to Dönitz, who in turn sent an up-date to his waiting wolf pack, Liebe made a rather half-hearted sortie, damaging only one ship. He then broke off the action. Shortly after Liebe had withdrawn on the morning of the 18th, the convoy escort was reinforced by the sloop HMS *Leith* and the corvette HMS *Heartsease*. The guard around SC 7 now consisted of 2 sloops and 2 Flower class corvettes, none of which, unfortunately, had experience of operating with the others. It was therefore a somewhat fragmented group. However, as the convoy was now only 150 miles from the west coast of Ireland and well within reach of air cover, there were grounds for optimism. But, at about 19.00 on the night of 18th, in fine clear weather, SC 7 sailed into the trap.

The least experienced of Dönitz's aces, Karl-Heinz Moehle, in *U-123*, opened the attack and all but bungled the whole thing. He fired at the 5,458-ton *Shekatika*, which was romping ahead of the convoy, but failed to sink the British ship. The more experienced Engelbert Endrass, in *U-46*, moved in quickly, before the escorts could coordinate their defence. The lookout on the bridge of the *Beatus* was the first to sight *U-46* as her low outline was silhouetted by the moonlight on the port bow. His cry of warning alerted Captain Brett, who just had time to order the transmission of the submarine attack warning (SSS) before the torpedo struck.

Endrass had aimed well. The torpedo caught the *Beatus* squarely amid-ships on her port side, causing rapid flooding of the engineroom and adjacent holds. A brief inspection of the chaos was enough to convince Brett that his ship was damaged beyond all salvation and would, in spite of her timber cargo, soon sink. He gave the order to abandon ship.

As so often happens when abandoning ship at night under such horrific circumstances, there was a certain amount of confusion. One lifeboat was lost through a panicking Asian fireman cutting through the rope falls with an axe but, fortunately, the boat was not yet manned and no lives were lost. The small jolly boat was pressed into service and Brett and his crew were able to get away safely.

Following the torpedoing of the *Beatus*, the convoy commodore ordered the other ships to scatter. The slaughter then began in earnest. With the corvette *Heartsease* having left to stand by the *Carsbreck*, damaged by *U-38* and *Scarborough* still some miles astern, the remaining escorts, two sloops and a corvette, could do little more than chase their tails while, manoeuvering on the surface with impunity, the U-boats

s/s *Beatus* 4885 GRT. Sunk by *U-46* in north Atlantic 18 October 1940.

s/s *Fiscus* 4885 GRT. Sunk by *U-99* in north Atlantic 18 October 1940.

moved in. In the next two and a half hours five more merchant ships were sunk and the *Shekatika* again damaged.

When the first fury of the battle had died away, the 2,118-ton Dutch ship *Boekolo*, commanded by Captain J. de Groot, decided to return to the convoy and, in doing so, came upon the two lifeboats containing Captain William Brett and the 27 men of the *Beatus*, which had taken forty minutes to sink. Making a very brave, but in retrospect, foolish decision, de Groot stopped his ship and made ready to pick up the survivors. The first boat from the *Beatus* was alongside when Joachim Schepke in *U-100* appeared on the scene and, without hesitation, put an end to de Groot's errand of mercy. Schepke's torpedo took the *Boekolo* in her No. 4 hold and, taking a heavy list to port, she began to settle quickly by the stern. *Beatus*'s mess boy, who had been the only man to board the *Boekolo* joined the Dutchmen in their boats.

Horrified by the unopposed destruction going on around him and still filled with the sense of foreboding that had been with him since before sailing from Three Rivers, Captain Ebenezer Williams pulled the heavily-laden *Fiscus* out of the convoy and rang for full revolutions. Under the circumstances prevailing his decision to make a run for it could not be challenged, for the tiny escort force of SC 7 was now completely overwhelmed. However, Williams had made his move too late, for the wily Otto Kretschmer was then moving in for his 25th kill of the war.

U-99's torpedo ripped open the hull plates of the *Fiscus* and, with all her reserve buoyancy cancelled out by the great weight of steel in her holds, she plunged to the bottom like a stone. Captain Ebenezer Williams and his 27-man crew, which included two Cardiff boys of fourteen and fifteen, went with her, sucked down into the raging maelstrom created by her sinking. The battle, if such a one-sided conflict could be so called, continued throughout the night of the 18th and into the early hours of the next day. Only when, at about 04.00 on the 19th, the U-boats had expended all their torpedoes, did they break off and fade away into the coming dawn. By this time Convoy SC 7 had lost 21 ships out of the 35 that had set sail from Cape Breton fourteen days earlier. Two more were badly damaged.

Captain Brett and the men of the *Beatus* were picked up by the corvette *Bluebell*, while the survivors of the *Boekolo*, including the *Beatus*'s mess boy, found safety in the sloop *Fowey*. All were landed at Gourock on the 20th. The third Welsh ship involved, Reardon Smith's *Botusk*, escaped not only the U-boats but a British minefield she inadvertently ran over while approaching the Scottish coast in fog. Ironically, she finally met her end in January 1944, sunk by a British mine off North Rona, Scotland.

The destruction of Convoy SC 7 was the first big action of the Battle of the Atlantic and should have been a salutary warning to the British Admiralty. To send convoys of small, slow and lightly escorted merchant ship across a North Atlantic seething with U-boats was folly enough in summer; in winter, as with SC 7, it was little short of ritual murder for the merchant seamen involved. Unfortunately, the lesson never really sank home.

As to those who, in this winter of 1940, sank the Red Dragon, Kapitän-Leutnant Engelbert Endrass was to lose his life in *U-567* when she was destroyed by the sloop HMS *Deptford* off the coast of Spain in December 1941. *U-46* faded into obscurity and was scuttled in May 1945. Korvetten-Kapitän Otto Kretschmer, the ace of all U-boat aces, lasted until March 1941 when, in *U-99*, he was caught by the destroyer HMS *Walker* while attacking Convoy HX 112 in the North Atlantic. *U-99* was sunk but most of her crew, including Kretschmer, were taken prisoner.

7

The Fresno City: Jervis Bay convoy

In the early winter of 1940, Britain, for the first time since Napoleon Bonaparte massed his invasion barges in the Channel ports, faced a serious threat of invasion. A decisive battle had been won in the air but Hitler's victorious army was still poised awaiting the opportunity to cross the English Moat. The whole emphasis of British air and sea reconnaisance was therefore now concentrated on the Channel and the Southern North Sea. The time was ideal for the German pocket battleship *Admiral Scheer* to break out into the Atlantic Ocean.

Launched in 1933 and only ready for service after the outbreak of war, the 10,000-ton *Admiral Scheer* carried, in addition to torpedoes and anti-aircraft guns, six 11-inch and eight 5.9-inch guns. She had a top speed of $26\frac{1}{2}$ knots and a range of 19,000 miles without refuelling. Commanded by Kapitän-zur-See Theodor Krancke, she left the Baltic on 23 October 1940 and reached the Atlantic via the Denmark Strait undetected. Krancke had orders to mount an attack on British convoys, many of which were now only lightly defended due to the withdrawal of Royal Navy ships to the Mediterranean following the Italian declaration of war.

The 4,955-ton *Fresno City*, registered in Bideford and owned by Sir William Reardon Smith of Cardiff lay at anchor at Sydney, Cape Breton, loaded to her Winter North Atlantic marks with 8,129 tons of Canadian maize. She was to form part of one of the largest and fastest convoys ever to cross the North Atlantic from west to east. In spite of the daunting prospect of a winter crossing, Captain R. L. Lawson had every confidence in his ship, which was well found in all respects, capable of a speed of 14 knots and carried the standard merchant ship armament of 4-inch and 12-pounder guns.

The rest of the assembled convoy, viewed through Lawson's binoculars, were a satisfying sight, smart looking ships all of them, including the New Zealand Shipping Company's 16,698-ton *Rangitiki* and several large tankers. The convoy commodore's ship was the *Fresno City*'s four-year old sister ship *Cornish City*, commanded by Captain John O'Neill. Lawson's confidence ebbed when he swung his binoculars onto the sole escort ship of Convoy HX 84. She was the 14,164-ton armed merchant cruiser *Jervis Bay*, an ex-Aberdeen and Commonwealth liner. Built in 1922, the AMC was armed with seven 5.9-inch guns – which were even older than herself – and had a top speed of only 15 knots. She was a sad reflection on Britain's naval strength at this stage of the war.

Convoy HX 84 sailed from Sydney, Cape Breton on the evening of 27 October, at about the same time as the *Admiral Scheer* was leaving Brunsbuttel to make her stealthy way north to the Denmark Strait. The *Fresno City* was comfortably stationed in the middle of the convoy, immediately astern of the *Jervis Bay*. Steering an east-southeasterly course, the ships made for a prearranged rendezvous in 41° N 43° W where, at first light on 2 November, they were joined by ships homeward bound from ports south of the Chesapeake River and from Canada's west coast. The merger resulted in a convoy of 38 ships carrying over a quarter of a million tons of vital cargo for a beleaguered Britain. There was no increase in the escort force. Settling down into nine columns covering ten square miles of ocean, HX 84 set a northeasterly course for the northwestern approaches to the British Isles, some 1,600 miles away.

At the same time, 450 miles to the southwest, the British refrigerated vessel *Mopan*, homeward bound from Jamaica with 70,000 stems of bananas, was pushing northeastwards at high speed. The *Mopan* crossed ahead of and in sight of HX 84 in the forenoon of the 5th, but did not exchange signals. The weather at the time was fine with excellent visibility and the *Mopan*'s 68-man crew no doubt felt a thrill of pride as their sleek ship raced across ahead of the convoy. Fifty miles or so to the north-east, the *Admiral Scheer* was searching for Convoy HX 84, which Kapitän Krancke had been advised was somewhere in the area. At just after 13.00 the *Mopan* sailed into his arms and Krancke stopped her with a couple of well-aimed shells.

The first reaction of the *Mopan*'s captain when his ship came under fire was to send a message warning the convoy of the enemy's presence. He was forestalled in this by Krancke, who threatened to blow the *Mopan* out of the water if her radio was used. By 16.00 the British cargo ship was a burning wreck and her crew in the lifeboats pulling clear. Had the *Mopan* been able to send out the customary RRR (Attacked by Raider) signal, HX 84 would have gained a small advantage that might have saved many lives, but it would not have escaped the *Admiral Scheer*, whose Arado reconnaisance plane had already sighted the smoke of the convoy.

Unaware of the approaching danger, HX 84 continued to steam steadily north-eastwards until, at 15.40, the *Rangitiki* signalled the Commodore in the *Cornish City* reporting smoke at four points on the port bow. At 17.00 the *Empire Penguin* signalled a ship approaching the convoy from a northerly direction. HX 84 was then in position 53° 50' N, 32° 15' W, about half way between Newfoundland and Ireland. Six minutes later, the *Fresno City*'s chief officer reported to Captain Lawson he had sighted what appeared to be a pocket battle ship on the port beam. As he was hurrying up the bridge ladder, Lawson heard the commodore's sound signal ordering an emergency turn to starboard. In convoy, this was a manoeuvre only resorted to in the event of imminent danger. Lawson reached the bridge just in time to see the first salvo from the *Admiral Scheer*'s 11-inch guns straddle the *Jervis Bay*, which was in the centre of the convoy, mid-way between the 4th and 5th columns. One of the shells demolished the forward funnel of the *Rangitiki*, leading the 6th column, while another appeared to hit the *Cornish City*, leader of the 5th column.

Lawson rang for emergency full speed and, with her engines working up to 14 knots and her helm hard to starboard, the *Fresno City* followed the other ships in putting her stern to the enemy. The merchant ship could do no more than make a run for it. As the *Fresno City* came around to starboard, Lawson watched with horror and admiration as the *Jervis Bay*, her guns firing, pulled out of the convoy and headed at full speed towards the *Admiral Scheer*. Captain E. S. Fogarty Fegen, the AMC's commander, his ship hopelessly outclassed in everything but the courage of himself and his crew, had no intention of allowing his convoy to be savaged.

The fight was hopelessly one-sided and soon over. Before the *Jervis Bay* could bring her 5.9's within range of the enemy, Lawson saw her hit on her port side, where fire broke out at once. The next 11-inch salvo from the *Admiral Scheer* took the unarmoured liner square in the bridge superstructure, starting another fire. Lawson shook his head sadly and turned away. He must look to his own ship.

The *Fresno City*'s gun's crew were closed up at her 4-inch stern gun and, more in a gesture of defiance than anything else, Lawson gave the order to open fire on the raider. Other ships in the convoy also opened fire but the range was too great, the *Admiral Scheer*, by this time, being six or seven miles astern. Smoke floats were dropped by the fleeing ships in an attempt to aid their escape, but these proved ineffective. The *Jervis Bay* was now burning furiously, her guns silent, but she had achieved what Fogarty Fegen had set out to do. The merchant ships had scattered and were steaming away from the raider at maximum speed. The unopposed massacre Krancke had looked for was not to be. Keeping his binoculars on the *Admiral Scheer*, who had now turned her guns on the fleeing *Rangitiki*, Lawson brought the *Fresno City* round onto a course of 270 degrees and steamed west into the gathering twilight.

Under cover of darkness, he intended to gradually assume a south-southwesterly course, in the hope of slipping around the stern of the raider.

The *Jervis Bay*, ablaze from end to end, her hull holed and her steering gear smashed, did not finally sink until 20.00. Captain Fogarty Fegen, badly wounded, and 185 of his gallant crew went down with her. The outcome of their fight had been wholly predictable. An elderly merchant ship, armed only with 5.9-inch guns left over from the nineteenth century, was no match for an 11-inch gun pocket battleship. She had simply not been able to bring her guns into range of the *Admiral Scheer* before being reduced to a burning hulk. Every man of her crew would have died, if it had not been for the Swedish cargo steamer *Stureholm*, which, with an outstanding display of courage and compassion, slipped back under the guns of the raider and snatched 68 men from the water. Three of these were unfortunately dead when picked up.

Meanwhile, the *Fresno City*, having only the 9,800-ton, London registered *Beaverford* in company, was making good progress to the south. The two ships were on slightly divergent courses, so that the distance between them was gradually widening. Astern, Captain Lawson could see the flames from the other ships caught by the raider's guns but, for the time being, it seemed that his ship and the *Beaverford* had got away. At 21.50, more than four hours after the convoy had scattered, the *Beaverford* which was on the *Fresno City*'s port beam at about ten miles, suddenly came under fire and burst into flames.

Unable to see the enemy, Lawson altered away from the *Beaverford* and, for the second time that night, rang for emergency full speed. With her pistons hammering out a mad tattoo and her hull shaking like an animal possessed, the *Fresno City* fled into the night. After about fifty minutes of frenzied steaming, she seemed to be completely alone on the ocean and Lawson breathed a cautious sigh of relief. He might just have well as held his breath for, at that moment, from a shadowy form unseen on the starboard quarter, a searchlight snapped on, bathing the *Fresno City* in brilliant light. Moving with the stealth and speed of a stalking leopard, the *Admiral Scheer* had caught up with the fleeing merchant ship and was about to pounce. The range was point blank – no more than 200 feet Lawson judged – so the killing was swift and precise. In rapid succession, seven shells crashed into the *Fresno City*, two into her engineroom, then one into each hold, working from forward. Her engine, which had been labouring valiantly, came to a sudden stop. Hatchboards, tarpaulins and beams were blown skywards and flames leapt from the hatches as the cargo ignited and began to burn fiercely. Lawson, who was in the starboard wing of the bridge and still blinded by the *Admiral Scheer*'s searchlight, came near to death when a heavy object, possibly a hatch beam, all but demolished the wing. Stunned, he reached for the button of the air whistle to sound boat stations. There was little to be done for the *Fresno City* now. The whistle gave no response, for the air lines had been cut in the savage bombardment. Lawson sent his Chief Officer below to muster all hands to the boats by word of mouth, then stood by the bridge until he was satisfied the way was clear off the ship. This took about five minutes, after which Lawson went to the boat deck to supervise the abandoning of the ship. To his amazement he found the deck deserted, with the port lifeboat gone and the starboard boat suspended from its forward fall, its bow five feet above the water and in danger of being smashed by the heavy swell running.

As there was nothing Lawson could do with the boat alone, he went in search of help. He found the engine-room ablaze and empty of life, the after accommodation yielded the same negative result. Moving amidships, he met up with Second Officer Gleghorn and nine men, who had been sheltering from the shrapnel in the saloon alleyways. Sending these men to secure the starboard lifeboat, Lawson went forward, where he discovered carnage. The shell fired by the *Admiral Scheer* into the forward hold had apparently exploded in the vacant space on top of the cargo, completely wrecking and setting on fire the crew's accommodation under the forecastle head. Ordinary Seaman Smith was dead and Able Seamen Mackie and Finnis were seriously injured. The Deck Boy, W. H. Lynn, who had been on look-out on the forecastle head, was missing.

Under the direction of Second Officer Gleghorn the remaining lifeboat was made secure. The injured were brought aft and, with great difficulty due to the swell, lowered to the boat and made as comfortable as possible. Only then was the *Fresno City* finally abandoned. The time was 21.30, exactly half an hour after the *Admiral Scheer*'s first shell had landed. Captain Lawson was last to leave the ship, after which the lifeboat was pulled clear, fighting for every inch gained against the swell and wind which threatened to smash the frail boat against the ship's side. Once out of danger, Lawson's first thought was to find the other lifeboat, which he hoped contained the rest of his crew. Within a few minutes, this was seen some way off to port lying to a sea anchor, but it was another two hours before the two boats were brought together. Lawson then paid out the sea anchor of his own boat and, for the next three hours, the two lifeboats lay hove to, rising and falling on the swell, while their mother ship continued to burn. Shortly after 02.00 on 6 November, Lawson's sea anchor carried away and the boats drifted apart, never to regain contact with each other.

By 04.00 the *Fresno City* was almost completely burned out. The flames began to subside and, for a while, she was visible only as a dark silhouette against the night sky. At 04.35 by Lawson's watch, the whole superstructure of the ship was seen to fall in on itself and the *Fresno City* slipped below the waves. Making the two injured men as comfortable as possible, Lawson now hoisted the lifeboat's sails and headed back towards the position where the convoy was first attacked – a distance of about eighty miles, he estimated. There he hoped a ship or ships might be searching for survivors of the previous night's attack. But when he reached this position, at about noon on the 7th, the sea was empty as far as the eye could see. There was nothing else for it but to sail eastwards where, some 900 miles away, lay the coast of Ireland.

A westerly gale blew up on the 8th, bringing with it a rough, tumbling sea, but Lawson's boat behaved well, running before the wind under a jib sail only. Shortly after dawn on the 9th, smoke was sighted on the horizon to the south-east. Lawson immediately altered course in this direction and soon the masts and funnel of a cargo ship could be seen. A few hours later, Lawson and his men were picked up by the Greek ship *Mount Taygetus*, having sailed a distance of 200 miles from the sinking of the *Fresno City*. Once aboard the Greek ship, commanded by Captain Samathrakis, the British seamen were treated with the utmost warmth and hospitality, the injured men Mackie and Finnis receiving particular attention.

The *Fresno City*'s other lifeboat was also eventually found, with all on board safe, so that the final tally of casualties in the Welsh ships was gratifying low. Despite the destruction caused by seven 11-inch shells and the subsequent confused abandonment of the ship, and despite the turbulent weather that followed, Lawson had only lost one man. Miracles *do* happen.

The rest of the Convoy HX 84 had also fared better than would have been expected. Due solely to the heroic actions of Fogarty Fegen and the men of HMS *Jervis Bay*, the convoy had been able to scatter effectively and the *Admiral Scheer*, for all her speed and big guns, was able to sink only four merchant ships, other than the *Fresno City*. The British tanker *San Demetrio*, loaded with 7,000 tons of petrol was set on fire and abandoned, but later she was reboarded by some of her crew and reached port with most of her precious cargo intact. Three days after the raider's attack, the 2,374-ton Swedish ship *Vingaland* was bombed by a Focke-Wulf and finally sunk by the Italian submarine *Marconi*. In all, 31 ships of Convoy HX 84 reached port safely. At the final reckoning, only 46,000 tons of shipping had been lost, but the loss of life was grievous, 206 merchant seamen and 186 men of the Royal Navy having perished.

As for the *Admiral Scheer*, she was to sink another 9 Allied merchant ships in the South Atlantic before returning to Kiel in April 1941. Thereafter, as a result of Hitler's increasing reluctance to risk his big ships, she did no more than skulk in the Norwegian fiords, posing a threat to the Russian convoys. In 1944 she was destroyed by Allied bombs while in drydock at Kiel.

8

Oswald Frederick Swayne

The shores of Cardigan Bay and, in particular, the peninsula of Pencaer, the southernmost arm of the bay, are steeped in Welsh history. This is the land of the ancient Celts who journeyed north from Iberia five hundred years before the birth of Christ. It is a land of Arthurian legend and setting of part of the Mabinogion, whose dark tales date from the dawn of this Celtic world. It is also a place of great beauty, of rolling, gorse-covered hills and rich, undulating pastures which sweep down to end in spectacular Ordovician cliffs that have faced the raging Atlantic for 1,000 million years. The warm waters of the Gulf Stream washing past the feet of these cliffs give to the peninsula a temperate climate of its own that has no equal in these British Isles. The yellow gorse blooms on the hillsides even in the depths of winter, summer sets the hedgerows ablaze with colour and the golden browns of autumn herald nothing worse than a temporary faltering of the ever-rising sap.

The small town of Goodwick, in the county of Pembrokeshire, shelters on the east side of the Pencaer Peninsula and overlooks the shores of Fishguard Bay, a mere indentation in the greater bay of Cardigan. At the beginning of this century, Goodwick was home only to fishermen and farmworkers, then, with the coming of the Great Western Railway in 1906, a vast transformation took place. Two million tons of rock were blasted out of the face of the peninsula to construct what was then – somewhat unfairly many would say – named Fishguard Harbour, after Goodwick's rival town on the other side of the bay. Goodwick then assumed importance as the terminus for the cross-channel ferries which began to sail daily between the harbour and the southern Irish ports of Cork and Rosslare. But, although a degree of prosperity came, and with it more people and more houses, Goodwick had no ambitions to expand indiscriminately. To this day it is still no more than part village, part town, a meeting place between farmland and the sea, and convenient stepping stone to the nearby shores of Ireland.

In the shadow of the ancient church of Manorowen, one and a quarter miles along the road from Goodwick towards St David's, where the smell of the sea vies strongly with the scent of the hedgerows, there reigns a peace which is beyond this world. Here, where headstones of lichened granite and polished twentieth century marble mingle beneath the stately yews, there is a poignant reminder of a Welsh merchant seaman who gave his life for his country on a dark, alien night in December 1940. Though his last resting place lies 600 miles away in the deep Atlantic, Oswald Frederick Swayne, son of Albert Frederick and Agnes Esther Swayne, is remembered still on the grave of those who bore him with the simple words, 'Lost at sea December 2nd 1940'.

Son of a seaman, grandson of a seaman, Oswald Swayne was born in Goodwick in May 1916 into a world in the grip of a terrible war. It was not an easy world to enter and one which was made even more difficult ten years later by the death of Oswald's father in a tragic accident. Agnes Swayne, left with five young children to rear, might have been forgiven if she had turned away from the seemingly impossible future facing her; the Welfare State was still twenty-two years and another war away. But Agnes was not a woman to shirk her responsibilities, however heavy. She found work, albeit menial, and counting the pennies carefully and meeting each obstacle fearlessly as it arose, she competently assumed the mantle of both mother and father to her children. The Swayne family lived frugally, but in godliness and cleanliness, there flourishing in their midst a love and happiness no money could buy. The near-idyllic surroundings in which they lived played no small part in their life of contentment.

Following the death of his father, Oswald, being the eldest of the three Swayne boys, assumed the role of head of the house. At ten he was a slim-built, thoughtful boy who took his new responsibilities seriously. A year later, when he was accepted for the County Grammar School in Fishguard, both Oswald and his mother were prepared for the sacrifices necessary for his education until the age of sixteen. For Agnes Swayne, with four other children to provide for, it was a desperate struggle, but she did not flinch. As it happened, the country was moving into the worst economic depression it had ever known and it was perhaps fortunate Oswald was to spend the next five years at the County School.

If the formative years of Oswald Swayne's life were difficult, they were lived to the full and in happiness. Certainly his peace of mind was not marred by events taking place across the North Sea in Germany, where 9 million unemployed and hyper-inflation were stifling democracy. The Austrian corporal, Adolf Hitler, promising stability and revenge for Germany's humiliation of 1918, was poised to take over this virile and restless nation. By the time Oswald was twenty, Hitler had swept aside yet another treaty and marched his troops into the Rhineland.

Although Hitler had little enthusiasm for submarine warfare, he could not ignore the lessons of the First World War, when the U-boats came within an ace of starving Britain into submission. Admiral Karl Dönitz, who had been a successful submarine commander in the Kaiser's War, used his knowledge to sway Hitler and, as early as 1930 was secretly training officers and men to form the basis of Germany's U-boat arm of the future. When Hitler signed the London Protocol denouncing submarine warface against merchant shipping in 1936, Dönitz had already given orders for the first new U-boat keels to be laid. He calculated that at least 300 boats would be needed to mount an effective blockade of the British Isles, but Hitler would not agree. He preferred to channel money into the new pocket battleships, with which he hoped to defeat the Royal Navy on the surface. Consequently, at the outbreak of war in 1939, Germany possessed only 57 U-boats. Fortunately, due to the perception of Admiral Dönitz, these were all comparatively new, of advanced design and manned by submariners at the peak of their training. Among them was a young kapitän-leutnant named Ernst Mengersen.

September 1939 found Oswald Swayne, now a self-assured, handsome young man of twenty-three, working as a mechanic at the Royal Naval Armament Depot, deep in the beautiful Nant-y-Bugail Valley. His younger brother George, having endured the rigours of HMS *Ganges* as a boy seaman, was at sea as a telegraphist with the Royal Navy, while the eldest of the Swayne girls had left home to become a nurse. Agnes Swayne, having successfully guided all her children through the trauma of early life without a father, had found regular employment as a stewardess on the cross-channel ferries sailing between Goodwick and Ireland. The Swayne family, although far removed from the lap of luxury, was experiencing a satisfying degree of hard-won prosperity.

Except for a predictable upsurge in patriotism, the outbreak of war did very little to disturb the tranquility of Goodwick and the surrounding countryside. Before long, however, the young men began to disappear into the Services, the vast majority of them, born and brought up within sight of the sea, joining the Royal and Merchant Navies. Oswald Swayne's work at the armaments depot was classed as a 'Reserved Occupation', giving him immunity from conscription into the forces, and he could well have shut his ears to the momentous events happening outside Pembrokeshire. His job was secure and reasonably well-paid he had a good home and he had started to court Penelope, the pretty young daughter of a local coastguard. But the talk of the war at sea was all around him. His brother was in the fighting ships, many of his close friends were also risking their lives to keep the sea-lanes open and, not least, his mother was quietly braving the dangers of the St George's Channel on a daily basis. Predictably, before the war was many months old, Oswald was talking to his mother about a career in the Merchant Navy. With his engineering background, he could enter as a junior officer, a job with status and good prospects of promotion. Agnes Swayne was perhaps more aware of the dangers of the war at sea than those around her and she feared for her son. She argued that, in his work at the Depot he was already serving his country, perhaps in a more useful way than he could do at sea. Her argument fell on deaf ears. In early January 1940, Oswald Swayne, handsome in the blue/black doeskin and brass buttons of a junior engineer officer in the Merchant Navy, said goodbye to his mother and family, kissed a tearful Penelope and boarded the train for Cardiff to take up an appointment with the Tatem Steam Navigation Company.

The Tatem Steam Navigation Company, of 113 Bute Street, Cardiff, was founded in 1910 by William James Tatem, whose roots, like many Welsh-based shipowners, were in the West Country. Tatem had first set up business in 1897 with one ship, the 2,950-ton *Lady Lewis*, which was commanded by William Reardon Smith, later to become the premier shipowner in Wales. Working on the charter market and shipping coal from South Wales to the River Plate and grain back to Europe, Tatem prospered and his one ship became a small fleet. For his services to his country in the First World War, he was created Baron Glanely of St Fagans. In 1939 the Tatem Steam Navigation Co. owned 12 ships, all except one named after towns and villages in Tatem's native Devon which ended with the suffix 'leigh', as in *Iddesleigh*, *Winkleigh*, *Chumleigh*, etc. The one exception, the *Lady Glanely*, was the flagship and pride of the Tatem fleet. Built in 1938 by William Doxford & Sons, the 5,497-ton *Lady Glanely* was a motor ship, one of the first South Wales' ships to depart from steam propulsion. She was also built with all her accommodation amidships in one block, a style not to attain general popularity until many years after the war. A ship before her time, the *Lady Glanely* was commanded by Captain Alexander Hughson, a fifty-eight-year old Shetland Islander.

On 8 January 1940, Junior Engineer Officer Oswald Swayne

joined the *Lady Glanely* at Cardiff and, within a few days had left behind the grey drizzle of winter in South Wales and was heading south into a kinder climate. The *Lady Glanely* was making her usual run to South America with coal and would return loaded to her marks with grain from the pampas of Argentina.

The five-month voyage began Oswald Swayne's education in the hard school of life. He was introduced to the strange new worlds that lay beyond the borders of Wales, he experienced the many moods of the sea and tasted the delights of alien shores. When he returned on leave to Goodwick in the summer of 1940, he came with a tan on his skin and his pale-blue eyes shining with a new zest for life. The leave was short, but long enough for this confident young sailor to make a commitment to the girl he had fallen in love with. He and Penelope became engaged and they made plans to marry at the conclusion of his next voyage. Oswald returned to the *Lady Glanely* in Cardiff, from where she would set sail in August, once more bound for South America.

9

The Lady Glanely: the wolves attack

Meteorological Office statistics record the winter
of 1940 as one of the worst winters in living
memory in the North Atlantic. Those who sail
this ocean on a regular basis would argue that
winter in the North Atlantic is always a bad experience. It
is one long, weary succession of depressions which, forming
off Cape Hatteras, constantly sweep across the great expanse
of open water from west to east. These depressions are not
merely local storms but huge areas of low pressure up to 1,000
miles across and with central pressures as low as 960 milibars.
In mid-Atlantic, where the systems reach the climax of their
power, winds blow up to 100 knots, the swell is long and mountainous with waves sometimes reaching 50 feet before they
topple to fill the air with driving, salt-laden spray. Marching
in company with the wind and the waves comes the rain; thick,
blanketing drizzle at first, then spasmodic, stinging showers,
cold and demoralizing. Winter North Atlantic is a miserable
time.

In that winter of 1940, British and Allied merchant ships
had much more to face than the familiar malevolence of the
weather. The German U-boats were in fully cry, organized
by Admiral Dönitz into 'wolf-packs', each with its own hunting
ground. When the existence of a convoy had been established
by Lorient, the word was flashed to the nearest wolf-pack,
which then fanned out and attempted to make contact. The
first U-boat to sight the convoy became a shadow to the unsuspecting merchant ships, homing the rest of the wolf-pack in
by radio. The concerted attack was usually made at night,

with the U-boats working on the surface where their speed often exceeded that of the convoy escorts. The result was often a dreadful blood-letting.

With the fall of France and the opening up of the Biscay coast to the U-boats, their numbers in the Atlantic increased dramatically. At the same time the Royal Navy was stretched by the Italian intervention in the war and there was an inevitable shortage of escorts for the Atlantic convoys. For many of the east-bound convoys – ships loaded with vital war supplies – the best they could expect for the greater part of the passage was the doubtful protection of an armed merchant cruiser. At a point about 600 miles to the west of Ireland, a change over of escorts with a westbound convoy usually took place, the AMC handing over to the destroyer and corvette escort group which had guarded the westbound convoy thus far. In theory, the eastbound ships then had maximum protection through the dangerous waters of the western approaches to the British Isles. Of course, under the conditions prevailing in winter, the interchange of escorts was anything but precise, one or both convoys often being left unprotected for a number of hours. If Eire had been willing to allow Britain the use of air bases on her west coast, this area could have been covered by long-range aircraft. However, although eagerly accepting goods brought across the Atlantic in British ships, the Irish were, in the words of Winston Churchill, 'quite content to sit happy and see us strangled'. At the same time there is evidence that the U-boats often used Irish harbours for shelter and supplies.

Such was the situation in the North Atlantic when the *Lady Glanely*, commanded by Captain Alexander Hughson, left Vancouver in early November 1940, heavily loaded and topped off with a deck cargo of timber. Junior Engineer Officer Oswald Swayne, still marvelling at the great emptiness of British Columbia – more than fifty times the size of Wales – looked forward to the coming voyage with little thought for the dangers it involved. In less than a month, the *Lady Glanely* would be arriving in London, her port of discharge, with

m/v *Lady Glanely* 5497 GRT. Torpedoed by *U-101* and lost with all hands 400 miles west of Bloody Foreland 2 December 1940.

Type VII-C U-boat entering harbour.

Kapitän-Leutnant Ernst Mengersen.

Christmas only three weeks away. Given the parsimonious rate of leave granted in merchant ships, he would be entitled to only six days at home after four months away but there would be time enough to take Penelope to the altar in St Peters. It would be a fitting end to his first year at sea.

The 4,000-mile passage from Vancouver to Balboa, at the Pacific end of the Panama Canal, was a pleasant twelve-day transfer from the Canadian winter to the sub-equatorial warmth of Panama Bay. After much of one day spent manoeuvering through the 42 mile-long canal, the *Lady Glanely* emerged into the deep blue of the Caribbean, an ocean paradise of hot days and warm nights under a velvet sky dripping with diamond-blue stars. It seemed so far removed from the hell of a North Atlantic winter that no man on board, except perhaps Captain Hughson, could believe that other world not only existed but was inexorably drawing them into its dark, frightening void.

Entering the Atlantic through the Windward Passage, they headed north-eastwards to Bermuda, where Convoy **BHX 90** – the southern section of HX 90 – was assembling. Off this coral-fringed outpost of the British Empire, the *Lady Glanely* was joined by one of her sister ships, the 5,448-ton *Goodleigh*, also owned by Tatems of Cardiff.

BHX 90 sailed from Bermuda on 19 November and steamed north-east for 1,200 miles in steadily deteriorating weather. On the 24th, in position 41°N, 43°W, the Bermuda convoy met and merged with a convoy originated at Halifax, Nova Scotia. The completed Convoy HX 90 consisted of forty ships, steaming in nine columns spaced five cables apart, and now included three more Welsh ships, the *Victoria City* and the *Quebec City* owned by Sir William Reardon Smith of Cardiff and the twenty-eight year-old *Botavon*, manned and managed by the same company for the Ministry of War Transport. The *Botavon* carried the Commodore of HX 90 and was commanded by Captain Henry Isaac. In the *Victoria City*, sailing as an apprentice, was Philip Reardon Smith, son of Captain John Henry Reardon Smith and great-nephew of Sir William. The Red Dragon was well represented in Convoy HX 90.

Incredible though it may seem in retrospect, this great armada of helpless merchant ships was to proceed across what was then deemed the most hazardous stretch of water in the world escorted only by one armed merchant cruiser, namely HMS *Laconia*.

The 19,695-ton ex-Cunard liner *Laconia* was one of the 50 passenger liners recruited into the Royal Navy early in the war to act as convoy escorts, thereby releasing the Navy's fighting ships for more offensive roles. The experiment was doomed from the start. The AMC's were slow, cumbersome, possessed no protective armour plating and were armed mainly with obsolete guns taken from scrapped warships. Matched against German capital ships, the *Rawalpindi* and the *Jervis Bay* were hopelessly outclassed on all counts but the supreme

88mm U-boat deck gun in action against surface target.

courage and self-sacrifice of their commanders and crew. Confronted by a determined U-boat attack, the AMC's, without asdic or depth charges, were not only useless in defence of the convoy but defenceless themselves. Before they were withdrawn from service in 1942, fifteen of these expensive and heavily manned vessels had been sunk.

Shortly after the *Lady Glanely* and the other Bermuda ships joined up with HX 90, the first of the Atlantic storms moved in and for forty-eight hours the convoy was battered by high winds and heavy seas. Station keeping was impossible, most of the deep-laden ships being able to do little more than maintain steerage way. One by one the less able dropped out until, by the morning of the 26th, when the weather had subsided, nine ships were missing, including the *Victoria City*. As there were no fast escorts available to round up the stragglers, the convoy re-formed as best it could and pressed on eastwards. The *Lady Glanely* was directed by the Commodore to take up position as leader of the port outside column, one of the most exposed spots in the convoy.

Even before HX 90 sailed from Halifax, the Admiralty had evidence to suggest that the route of the convoy had been leaked to the Germans by sources in Canada. It can be understood why this knowledge was withheld from the captains of the merchant ships but there can be no conceivable excuse for not changing the convoy's route after sailing. This was not done and the consequences were dire, for Admiral Dönitz had some of his best men at sea.

While HX 90 was reeling under the storm of 24th/26th, one thousand miles to the east the alterted U-boats were setting up an ambush. Forming up in an extended north-south line in the path of the convoy were top-scoring ace Otto Kretschmer in *U-99*, Günther Prien, idol of the German public, in *U-47*, Herbert Kuppisch in *U-94*, Otto Salman in *U-52*, Gerd Schreiber in *U-95*, Hans-Peter Hinsch in *U-140*, Wolfgang Lüth in *U-43* and the young Ernst Mengersen in *U-101*. Weather conditions for the projected amubush were almost perfect. A force 4 to 6 wind gave waves high enough to make the trimmed-down U-boats difficult to see without seriously impeding their progress. Visibility after dark was excellent, with a bright moon until about 20.00 and brilliant Northern Lights throughout the night. Unknown to the U-boat commanders – or perhaps it was – they were to be handed another great advantage.

In accordance with Admiralty practice, HX 90 was due to exchange escorts with the westbound Convoy OB 251 on the morning of 2 December in longitude 17 degrees west. HMS *Laconia* was to return westwards with OB 251, while the destroyers *Vanquisher* and *Viscount*, the sloop *Folkestone* and the corvette *Gentian* would leave OB 251 and take over the shepherding of HX 90 to the UK. As the two convoys would pass on parallel and opposite courses at about ninety miles apart, the change-over of escorts could not be simultaneous, but it was hoped the gap would be minimal. At the best, this was an arrangement fraught with danger, in the event, it turned out to be a disaster for HX 90, and for the Welsh ships in particular.

At 07.00 on the morning of 1 December, with HX 90 maintaining steady progress to the east at $9\frac{1}{2}$ knots, the Belgian ship *Ville D'Arlon* developed steering gear trouble and dropped out of the convoy. This was a common enough occurrence in a convoy of merchant ships, many of whom were old and lacking in maintenance. On this occasion, the straggling of the Belgian ship in daylight was to set in motion a tragic and bloody chain of events. Throughout the previous night, Kapitän-Leutnant Ernst Mengersen, in *U-101*, had been scouting ahead of the wolf-pack but had made no sighting of the convoy, which was actually to the south of his search area. After daylight on the 1st, Mengersen decided to search to the south-east and, in doing so, missed HX 90, for the massive assembly of ships had already crossed ahead of him and was over the horizon by the time he reached their latitude. Unfortunately for HX 90 and providentially for Mengersen, on the afternoon of the 1st he sighted the *Ville D'Arlon*, which was now again under way and steaming after the convoy at full speed. Mengersen tucked his U-boat in behind the Belgian ship and sent a sighting report to his waiting companions.

The *Ville D'Arlon*, with *U-101* in close attendance, rejoined HX 90 at 17.00 on the 1st, at the same time as HMS *Laconia* said her farewells and left to join Convoy OB 251. The weather was fine with the wind blowing west-southwest force 6 and darkness was drawing in. HX 90, forty loaded merchant ships, was steaming east-northeast at $9\frac{1}{2}$ knots without escort and without any naval control, other than that exercised by the Commodore in the *Botavon*. Mengersen manoeuvred *U-101* into position on the starboard side of the convoy and waited for the moon to set. At 20.15 he fired a fan of three torpedoes, hitting first the 8,826-ton British tanker *Appalachee* and one minute later, the 4,958-ton *Loch Ranza*. The third torpedo missed.

The convoy was now less than 300 miles to the west of Ireland and it may have been for this reason a certain amount of complacency had settled over the ships. Heavy rain had begun to fall. The explosions of Mengersen's torpedoes were heard on the bridge of the *Botavon* and confused lights seen in the direction of the starboard wing of the convoy some three miles off, but no wireless distress messages were picked up or distress rockets seen. The Commodore, who had not been on the bridge at the time of the explosions, wrongly concluded that the sounds were thunder and the lights signals between ships which had come near to colliding in the rain squall. He took no action.

Out on the starboard wing of the convoy, apparently unseen, the *Appalachee* was sinking, while the *Loch Ranza*, herself damaged, was picking up survivors from the tanker. Both ships fell back into the darkness as the convoy continued on its unsuspecting way. Mengersen, who may not have been aware that HX 90 was now unescorted, had withdrawn to a safe distance but was still in contact with the convoy.

At 01.00 on the morning of the 2nd, the convoy altered course to approach the pre-arranged rendezvous with the escorts coming from OB 251. Thirty minutes later, the *Ville D'Arlon* again experienced a steering gear fault and prepared to once more drop astern. In doing so, she hoisted the customary 'Not Under Command' signal of two red lights. However, these lights were not dimmed, as they should have been in wartime and were, in fact, so bright that they could be seen by every ship in the convoy. If any of the U-boat wolf-pack, called in by Mengersen, had any doubts about the position of the convoy, they were soon dispelled by the *Ville D'Arlon*'s lights. Forty minutes later, Günther Prien, in *U-47*, put a torpedo into the Belgian ship and she sank quickly taking with her the brilliant marker lights, and all her unfortunate crew. But the damage had been done. The unprotected HX 90 was now pin-pointed and the rest of the pack was moving in for the kill.

A massacre followed. The U-boats, unrestrained by the danger of retaliation, their helpless targets illuminated by the Northern Lights, slipped in amongst the slow moving columns of merchantmen and ranged up and down, torpedoing at will and using their deck guns when their tubes were empty. The convoy's only defence lay in a series of emergency turns, by which it was hoped to spoil the enemy's aim. The Commodore of HX 90 was later to say: 'I could not keep track of all the emergency turns as sometimes we had barely finished one when we had to go off again. We were like a helpless flock of sheep in a narrow lane with a dog on each side.'

In hindsight, it might have been far wiser for the unescorted ships to scatter at first sign of a concerted attack rather than to stay bunched up together sharing each other's agony. Most certainly, Captain Alexander Hughson in the *Lady Glanely* would have been well advised to break away on his own. The *Lady Glanely* was a powerful motorship, only two years old, and, under pressure, she would have been capable of at least 15 knots, perhaps more. But the discipline of the convoy, instilled into merchant captains by dogmatic naval theorists over two wars, was too great. Hughson continued to hold his position as leader of the port wing column with his engine ticking over at a little more than half speed.

Just after 03.00, Ernst Mengersen, having reloaded his tubes, positioned *U-101* abreast the leading ships of the port wing of the convoy. At 03.20 the *Lady Glanely* moved into his sights and he fired. The torpedo took the Welsh ship squarely amidships. Eight minutes later, Captain Hughson ordered his wireless operator to transmit the SSS signal and then fired white distress rockets from the wing of the bridge. Mengersen, still on the surface, and able to aim and fire at his leisure, now torpedoed the 8,376-ton tanker *Conch*, next astern of the *Lady Glanely*. Then he turned his sights on the 3,862-ton steamer *Dunsley*, the last ship in the column.

On the bridge of the *Dunsley*, her master Captain J. Braithwaite heard the explosion and saw the white distress rockets arc up from the *Lady Glanely*. He immediately altered course hard to starboard and, in doing so, avoided Mengersen's third torpedo. Braithwaite now made a very brave and humane decison, one which was contrary to the convoy rules but in true Nelson tradition. Ignoring the obvious presence of the U-boats, he steered at full speed for the position of the torpedoed *Lady Glanely*, hoping he might be able to pick up survivors. It was not to be. At 03.50 Braithwaite sighted the lifeboats of the *Lady Glanely*, which had now sunk. He rang for slow speed and, twenty minutes later, the *Dunsley* was approaching the boats ready to pick up the survivors. At this point, *U-47*, commanded by Korvetten-Kapitän Günther Prien, who had sunk the battleship HMS *Royal Oak* with the loss of 833 lives in October 1939, intervened.

Braithwaite, occupied with manoeuvring his ship close to the *Lady Glanely*'s lifeboats, was informed of the sighting of a surfaced U-boat on the port beam at about half a mile, clearly visible in the flare of the Northern Lights. *U-47* opened fire with her 88 mm deck gun and Braithwaite, not a man to be intimidated, ordered his 4-inch gun's crew to return the fire. The fight was predictably one-sided. Although the *Dunsley*'s gunners claimed a hit on the submarine, she herself hit five times and caught fire. Loath though he was to leave the lifeboats, Braithwaite's first duty was to his own crew. He abandoned the rescue mission and, putting his ship stern on to *U-47*, steamed away at full speed, zig-zagging to avoid the shells still bursting around him.

There would be no more help for the men of the *Lady Glanely*, for the attack on the convoy was rising to a fierce crescendo. When the destroyer *Viscount* and a Sunderland flying boat searched the area on the morning of the 3rd, the lifeboats had disappeared. No one, it seems, will ever know what happened to those thirty-one merchant seamen, Oswald Swayne amongst them, on that terrible night in the North Atlantic.

The slaughter of Convoy HX 90 continued. At 05.15 the 2,782-ton *Kavak* was torpedoed on her starboard quarter and blew up. At about the same time, the tiny 1,586-ton *Tasso* was also sunk. The remaining Welsh ship, the 5,448-ton *Goodleigh*, sister ship of the *Lady Glanely*, was then the victim of a savage attack carried out by two U-boats. Günther Prien, who had condemned the survivors of the *Lady Glanely* to death, fired the first torpedo at the *Goodleigh* hitting her on the starboard side in way of the bridge, creating havoc in the wheelhouse and destroying the starboard wing. With the ship settling in the water, Captain Quaite, who had been injured by the explosion, gave the order to abandon ship. While this operation was in progress, Otto Kretschmer in *U-99* approached the disabled ship and added three more torpedoes, the last of which caused the *Goodleigh*'s 4-inch magazine to explode. Despite her terrible wounds, the Welsh ship, which was fully loaded with timber, stayed afloat for several hours, allowing all her crew, except her chief officer, who was probably killed in the attack, to get away in the boats. Later in the morning they were picked up by the destroyer *Viscount* and were landed at Liverpool on the 5th.

The Reardon Smith ship *Victoria City*, which had dropped out of the convoy on 26 November due to the bad weather, was never seen again and it is believed she was sunk by Hans-Peter Hinsch in *U-140*. Wreckage identified with her was washed up on the Irish coast on 8 December but of her 43 crew, including Apprentice Philip Reardon Smith, there was no trace.

HX 90's escort force finally arrived as the wintery sun was rising on the morning of the 2nd. The ragged remains of the convoy re-formed and continued on its way eastwards. But the agony was not over for the merchant ships, now struggling against a southwesterly gale. A far-ranging Focke-Wulf Condor sighted the convoy and at 10.00, attacked, bombing and

sinking the 4,360-ton *W. Hendrick* and wounding two
men on board the *Quebec City* with machine gun fire. That
afternoon, Otto Kretschmer in *U-99* and Herbert Kuppisch
in *U-94* returned and, despite the efforts of the hard-
pressed escorts, sank the 6,022-ton *Stirlingshire* and the
Norwegian ship *Samanger* of 4,276 tons. Later, after dark,
Kuppisch came back for what was to be the final assault on
the convoy, sinking the 6,725-ton Glasgow registered ship
Wilhelmina.

When it was all over, the reckoning could be done. Convoy
HX 90 had been under almost continuous attack for twenty-six
hours, most of this time completely unprotected by the Royal
Navy. A total of 11 ships of nearly 60,000 tons had been lost
and 3 ships damaged. For the U-boats, who apparently suffered
no casualties, it was a cheap victory and a victory of the first
magnitude. For the merchant seamen who survived it had
been a fearful nightmare they would have to live with for the
rest of their lives. For the dead, there was nothing but a cold,
unmarked grave.

The ships of the Red Dragon had taken a terrible beating.
Of the 5 ships involved in HX 90, 3 had been lost and 75
men were presumed dead. The fires were well banked in
Goodwick and the talk was of approaching Christmas when
the Atlantic wind moaned in over the Pencaer peninsula
bringing news of the loss of the *Lady Glanely*. A tight-lipped
Agnes Swayne was called to the telephone in Fishguard Harbour to be informed by a dispassionate Cardiff voice
that her son, Junior Engineer Officer Oswald Frederick
Swayne was missing following the loss of his ship by enemy
action.

The war was kinder to Ernst Mengersen. In *U-101*, and
later in *U-607*, he sank a further 58,361 tons of Allied shipping
and eventually received the Knight's Cross and promotion
to Korvetten-Kapitän. He survived to see the surrender of
the U-boats and he still lives in West Germany.

Günther Prien, whose intervention in the *Dunsley*'s rescue
bid led to the deaths of the men of the *Lady Glanely*, was not

so fortunate. After a five-hour duel with the destroyer *Wolverine* off Rockall on 7 March 1941, *U-47* was caught by a salvo of 10 depth charges and blew up under water. Prien and all his men perished. For the *Lady Glanely*, justice had been seen to be done.

10

The Grelrosa: against two enemies

January 1941 was the month of the Focke-Wulf Condor in the Battle of the Atlantic. Since the previous summer the Germans had been using these giant aircraft, with their range of over 2,000 miles, as scouts for the U-boat Arm, spotting and shadowing convoys from a safe distance while homing the U-boats in by radio. With Britain unable to provide air cover for her ships in the Atlantic, the Condors then assumed a more aggressive role, searching out and bombing convoy stragglers and merchant ships sailing independently. In January 1941 they sank 20 Allied ships of 78,517 tons.

Halifax, the capital of Nova Scotia, sits on a peninsula overlooking two magnificient deep-water bays. The outer bay, sheltered from the rigours of the Atlantic, is ten miles square and free from ice all the year round, making it, in 1941, the ideal North American assembly point for convoys bound for the British Isles. In this sheltered haven on 12 January of that year twenty-five merchant ships lay tugging at their anchors awaiting the signal to begin their battle with the dangers, natural and man-made, which lay beyond the headland. This was Convoy SC 19, scheduled to cross the North Atlantic at $7\frac{1}{2}$–8 knots, weather permitting – and in January it rarely did. Among the ranks of SC 19 were three Welsh ships, the 4,574-ton *Grelrosa* of the Cardigan Shipping Company, Tatem's *Winkleigh*, successor to the ship of that name sunk in the first week of the war, and the *West Wales*, owned by Gibbs & Co. (West Wales Shipping Co.).

Being escorted only by the armed merchant cruiser HMS

Aurania, an ex-passenger ship of 13,984 tons, the odds against SC 19 surviving the Atlantic passage seemed high, for German naval activity in these waters was at a peak. The 11-inch gun pocket battle ship *Admiral Scheer*, which had caused havoc in Convoy HX 84 two months earlier, and the 18,200-ton cruiser *Admiral Hipper* were both at large and, augmenting the usual complement of U-boats were eight Italian long range submarines. To all this was added the increasing threat of the Focke-Wulf Condors.

For Captain C. F. Linton of the *Grelrosa*, pocket battleships and U-boats were mere incidental dangers. His twenty-seven year-old ship was loaded down to her marks with a full cargo of wheat and he was in no doubt that the North Atlantic weather would be his greatest adversary once he put to sea. From early morning on the 12th he had anxiously watched the barometer falling and felt the wind freshening from the east. A depression was on its way up from Cape Hatteras. By late afternoon, when the convoy was preparing to sail, it was blowing a full gale, even in the shelter of the bay. Outside the headlands, the hounds of Hell were being let loose. With night coming on, Linton's seaman's instinct urged him to postpone sailing until next morning, and indeed he would have done so had the choice been solely his. The Canadian pilot who boarded the *Grelrosa* to take her out of harbour was of the same opinion and, after conferring with Linton, returned ashore to put their joint views to the Naval Control. Characteristically, the Navy brushed aside the opinions of the two merchant seamen, which were based on a thorough understanding of the power of the sea and the limitations of low powered merchant ships. Regardless of the weather, the convoy would sail that afternoon. It was a decision the Admirals would regret.

Convoy SC 19 sailed from Halifax at 16.00 on 12 January. Once clear of the headlands, the ships ran into the full force of an easterly gale, which threatened to blow them back into the bay. The light was already fading and the visibility was seriously reduced by driving snow. An attempt was made to form up the convoy in its predetermined nine columns but the weather was such that this was largely a pointless exercise. When darkness fell, SC 19 was still a jumble of hard-pressed ships, battered by heavy seas and, with the visibility at five cables, more occupied with avoiding collision with each other than with the irrelevant business of assuming tidy formation. During the night the gale backed to the northwest, with no abatement. By morning, with the visibility still hampered by snow squalls, the convoy appeared to have settled down into three widely scattered groups, the *Grelrosa* finding herself in company with five others. In between squalls, Linton caught sight of the leading ships of the convoy and decided to make a determined effort to catch up with them. The ageing *Grelrosa*'s best speed in fine weather was 8 knots but, in the conditions prevailing, the task Linton set her was beyond her capability. By the afternoon of the 14th she had not only failed to join the leaders but, with the driving snow showers merging into a continuous white curtain reducing visibility near to zero, she had lost all contact with the other ships.

At the Commodore's conference prior to sailing, Linton had been provided with the convoy route and various rendezvous positions to make for should he become separated from the convoy. He now had no option but to proceed independently, making for each rendezvous point in turn with the hope of eventually rejoining the main body of ships. There was no let up in the weather and, as the *Grelrosa* edged doggedly to the northeast, the temperature fell steadily. Ice began to form on deck and around the accommodation, adding discomfort to the fiendish, neverending punishment meted out by the pounding waves and heaving swell. Sextants were kept handy but it seemed the sun and stars had disappeared forever and all navigation was reduced to dead reckoning. For the first three days, Linton took comfort from wireless messages occasionally heard coming from the *Aurania* but the transmissions began to fade and he could only assume the *Grelrosa* was gradually falling further astern. But Linton had underestimated the capabilities of his ship. Convoy SC 19, having gathered in nineteen ships under its skirts was making good

s/s *Grelrosa* 4574 GRT. Bombed and sunk by Focke-Wulf Condor 400 miles west of Malin Head 28 January 1941.

an average speed of only 5½ knots, compared with the *Grelrosa*'s 6 knots. In the poor visibility the *Grelrosa* had actually overtaken the convoy and was steadily drawing ahead.

For another eight days the foul and miserable weather continued without let-up and the *Grelrosa* plodded on alone. Then, on the 25th, the weather at last began to moderate. By the 28th, when the Welsh ship was 200 miles from the west coast of Ireland, the wind and sea dropped away and the sun shone fitfully out of a cloudy sky. His ship having suffered and survived the worst the North Atlantic could throw at her, Linton was able to turn his mind to the other dangers which would inevitably threaten in the next forty-eight hours. The *Grelrosa* was now in the north-western approaches to the British Isles, waters infested with predatory U-boats and within easy reach of German long range bombers based in Western France. His ship was slow and ungainly and would be unable to run away from trouble. Her only defence lay in her armament, a 12-pounder high/low angle gun forward, a 4-inch anti-submarine gun aft and two Hotchkiss machine guns on the bridge. Her heavier guns were manned by DEMS gunners, who could be relied on to give a good account of themselves, if the opportunity arose. It only remained to keep a sharp lookout for danger.

It came at 10.00 on the morning of the 28th, when the *Grelrosa*'s Second Officer, who had the morning watch, sighted an aircraft flying low over the water on the port bow. Unable to identify the plane as friend or foe, he prudently sounded the pre-arranged signal for aircraft attack on the steam whistle. Captain Linton reached the bridge before the sound of the whistle had died away. He saw the aircraft circling at some distance from the ship. It was a four-engined, black-painted machine that looked only too familiar and ominous to Linton. He ordered the guns to be manned, telling his men to hold their fire until the plane made an obvious move towards the ship. Hardly had Linton's orders been carried out than the Focke-Wulf Condor, which he had now recognized it to be, came roaring in at mast top height, its bomb doors gaping open.

The *Grelrosa*'s 12-pounder opened up with a sharp crack but after getting away two rounds, the gunners were forced to cease fire, as the Focke-Wulf was already below the maximum depression of their gun. Unharmed, the enemy approached from the port quarter, spraying the bridge with his forward turret and releasing a bomb as he crossed the after deck from port to starboard. There was a heavy explosion and Linton, crouching behind the bulwark of the bridge wing, watched grim-faced as the *Grelrosa*'s mainmast toppled and fell, taking with it all the ship's aerials. The Focke-Wulf then circled briefly astern and came in for a second attack, sweeping across the ship in a fore and aft line. Three more bombs rained down, the first crashing through the engineroom skylight completely wrecking the engineroom, the second hit the cross-bunker hatch, burying itself in the coal before exploding, while the third bomb fell harmlessly into the sea on the port side of the bridge.

As the big, black aircraft roared over the length of the helpless ship, its fore and after turrets raked the decks and superstructure. The fire was returned by the bridge Hotchkiss guns, manned by the *Grelrosa*'s Third and Second Officers, while the 12-pounder was able to get off five rounds, one of which was seen to burst in front of the plane. Linton saw his Third Officer die, cut down by his own ammunition when the enemy's bullets exploded amongst it. Perhaps damaged or perhaps satisfied with the carnage it had wrought, the Focke-Wulf flew off towards the far horizon.

The *Grelrosa* was listing to starboard and settling bodily in the water and it required only a brief examination to convince Linton she was finished, her engine smashed, her hull plates holed. His Third Officer was dead, his Chief Engineer badly wounded and two men missing. He did what he could to make the injured men comfortable and ordered the rest of his crew to prepare to abandon ship. This was not to be the simple operation practiced at weekly boat drills. The bomb which had wrecked the *Grelrosa*'s engineroom had also torn her two lifeboats from their davits and hurled them into the water, where they now floated alongside, half-submerged. Fortunately, the *Grelrosa* carried two small jolly boats – little more than dinghys – one each side of the bridge. Linton ordered these two to be lowered and provisioned from the smashed lifeboats. The one remaining serviceable liferaft was also put over the side. While this was being done, the ship's wireless operator, P. T. O'Keith, rigged a jury aerial and, using the portable lifeboat transmitter, attempted to get away a distress message.

When the boats were ready, Linton ordered O'Keith to leave with the rest of the crew but the wireless operator refused to go until he was sure his SOS had been heard. The *Grelrosa*'s chief steward, A. Burn, who was doing his best to comfort the injured engineers, neither of whom could be moved, also refused to go to the boats. Linton, who had already decided he would not leave the injured men while the ship floated, pleaded with O'Keith and Burn to save themselves but the two officers shook their heads and carried on with their work. The ship was now listing heavily and Linton feared she would soon capsize. Eventually, the situation solved itself. O'Keith succeeded in transmitting an SOS and, at the same time, the gravely injured chief engineer died. Linton and the two officers then put the injured Third Engineer on a damaged raft, hoping he would float off when the ship sank, and finally abandoned the ship at 11.30. The *Grelrosa* went down half an hour later.

Linton split up his remaining men between the two small boats and the one serviceable raft. The jolly boats were leaking and badly overcrowded but, fortunately the sea was quiet. The Third Engineer was taken from his raft when it floated clear and made as comfortable as possible in one of the boats, but he died soon afterwards. There being no room elsewhere for Linton and Burn, they climbed onto one of the waterlogged lifeboats.

The bravery and persistence of Radio Officer P. T. O'Keith, who had refused to leave the ship until he had alerted the outside world to their fate, was rewarded next morning by the arrival of the destroyer HMS *Volunteer*. All 31 survivors of the *Grelrosa* were picked up and safely landed at Greenock.

The rest of Convoy SC 19 did not escape unscathed. The Focke-Wulf responsible for sinking the *Grelrosa* on the 28th informed Lorient of the position of the main body of the convoy and, at about 03.00 on the 29th, the U-boats moved in. In quick succession *U-93*, commanded by Kapitän-Leutnant Clause Korth, torpedoed and sank three ships, including the 10,468-ton British tanker *W. B. Walker*, before being chased off by the destroyers which had arrived to shepherd SC 19 into the North Channel.

At this time, the 4,354-ton *West Wales* was wallowing along twelve miles astern of the convoy. Like her elderly sister, the *Grelrosa*, she had had no contact with SC 19 since shortly after leaving Halifax. At about 05.00, she was sighted by Herbert Kuppisch, in *U-94*, who had been frustrated in his efforts to attack SC 19. One torpedo into the starboard side of the *West Wales* was sufficient to stop her dead in her tracks and set her sinking by the bow. Captain Frederick Nicholls ordered his men to the boats at once. As the boats were being lowered, Kuppisch fired a second torpedo from a range of about 100 yards and the crippled Welsh ship sank almost immediately, leaving many of her crew struggling in the icy water.

When a destroyer arrived on the scene about ten minutes later, it was able to pick up seventeen men from the lifeboats. A second destroyer subsequently rescued Captain Nicholls and four of his men from the water, but Nicholls died on board the naval ship soon after being picked up. Of the *West Wales*'s crew of 37, sixteen men died on that cold January morning 120 miles to the southwest of the lonely Atlantic island they call Rockall.

U-94 escaped the attentions of the destroyers and lived to create more havoc amongst Allied shipping. She was eventually sunk in a combined operation by the Canadian destroyer *Oakville* and aircraft of the US Squadron 92 off the West Indies in August 1942. Kuppisch was not in command at the time. His final reckoning came a year later when, on 27 August

1943, he was lost with the auxiliary tanker *U-847* when she was sunk by aircraft from the US carrier *Card* some 300 miles to the west of the Azores. The other Welsh ship in SC 19, the *Winkleigh*, although also a straggler, escaped unharmed and was to survive the war.

11

The Nailsea Lass: the straggler

In the early months of 1941, the noose thrown around the British sea lanes by the U-boats was tightening relentlessly. The accumulative total of Allied shipping lost had reached 4,750,000 tons and the upward trend seemed unstoppable. Ships were now being sunk faster than replacements could be built and, for the nation whose survival in the war required the annual importation of 43 million tons of cargo, time was surely running out.

The first day of February opened with the sinking in the North Atlantic of the 4,351-ton Greek ship *Nicolaos Angelos*, announcing the return to the sea of Kapitän-Leutnant Herbert Schultze and *U-48* after an absence of almost twelve months. Schultze, whose first victim had been the *Winkleigh*, owned by Tatems of Cardiff, torpedoed within a few days of the outbreak of war, was now one of Germany's most successful U-boat commanders. The despatch of the *Nicolaos Angelos* brought his score to almost 95,000 tons. One more decent sized ship sent to the bottom would see him past the magical 100,000 ton mark, and must surely lead to the award of the long overdue Knight's Cross on his return to Germany. This heartening prospect must have been high in Schultze's mind as he cruised south-southeast towards the Western Approaches.

Two days before the sinking of the *Nicolaos Angelos*, and 3,000 miles to the south, Convoy SLS 64 was assembling at an anchorage in the shadow of the densely forested hills of Sierra Leone. SLS 64 was a slow convoy, with a planned speed of only $7\frac{1}{2}$ knots and an estimated passage time of nineteen days from Freetown to Oban, where the ships would join coastal convoys for their various ports of discharge. As if the disadvantage of speed was not handicap enough, SLS 64 was also to be completely unescorted and was therefore little more than a gesture of solidarity between the twenty merchantmen involved. Perhaps the Admiralty, in its wisdom, preferred the ships to take their chance in company rather than alone.

Among those about to enjoy the privilege of the doubtful security of Convoy SLS 64 was the twenty-four year-old *Nailsea Lass*, a steamer of 4,289 tons owned by Evans and Reid Management Co. of Cardiff. This ship had left Newport, Mon., in April of the previous year and was now, nine months later, on her way home with 6,200 tons of produce from India. It had been a long voyage and no one was more pleased to be about to embark on the final leg than Captain Thomas Bradford. But, while he was not averse to accepting the hospitality of the convoy, he had serious doubts about his ship's ability to keep pace with the others. She had seen her best years and she was a long time out of drydock, her bottom being badly fouled by weed and shell which had its origins in the warm waters of the East. At the very best, Bradford estimated, she might be able to make 7 knots on the passage north; with a head wind, which was to be expected at this time of the year, a lot less. The possibility of sailing independently must have occurred to Bradford but, as it turned out, the choice was to be made for him.

While the *Nailsea Lass* sweltered in the lee of Cape Sierra Leone, the 8-inch gun cruiser *Admiral Hipper* was at her berth in the Biscay port of Brest, preparing to embark on her second sortie of the war. Her first adventure had almost ended in disaster when, on Christmas Day 1940, she had been badly mauled while attacking a heavily escorted troop convoy off the Azores. Subsequent to this debacle, the heavy cruiser, which had a notoriously low cruising range for her size, had been limited to carrying out short patrols in the vicinity of her refuelling rendezvous, some 1,000 miles west of the Bay of Biscay. When she left Brest in early January, it was with orders to attack only lightly escorted convoys or merchant ships sailing alone.

Convoy SLS 64 left Freetown on the morning of 30 January, an organized assembly of ships but without the real means to defend itself against a determined foe. Most of the ships were armed, but only with the usual assortment of obsolete relics from the First World War. The *Nailsea Lass* was no exception to the rule, her quiver of arrows containing an ancient 4-inch, two Lewis guns and a strange device known as a Holman Projector. The product of the fevered imagination of a well-intentioned but somewhat naïve boffin, the Holman Projector was a crude form of mortar, connected to the ship's deck steam line and designed to fire hand grenades at low-flying aircraft. A merchant ship's deck steam being a most unpredictable form of propulsion, the grenade usually fell back to explode on deck after climbing 20 or 30 feet in the air. The projector's only real claim to utility lay in providing amusement for bored gunners, who used it to fire potatoes at adjacent ships in the convoy.

Captain Bradford's fears about his ship's ability to maintain the convoy speed were soon realized. In spite of the determined efforts of the *Nailsea Lass*'s engineers, the barnacles on her hull soon held her back and, by nightfall on the first day at sea, she was straggling astern. When dawn broke on 1 February, the convoy had disappeared over the horizon. Philisophically, Bradford accepted that he was now committed to sailing home alone and consoled himself with the thought that his ship was probably as safe on her own as she would be in the company of the unescorted convoy, if not safer. He was right. Thirteen days out of Freetown, when passing 150 miles east of the Azores, SLS 64 was pounced upon the waiting *Admiral Hipper*. In a very short space of time, like a savage wolf let loose amongst a flock of un-shepherded sheep, the 8-inch gun cruiser sank 7 ships, totalling 32,806 tons. She might well have taken her bloodied fangs to the rest of the fleeing convoy but she was again running short of fuel and was forced to return to Brest.

Unaware of her providential escape, the *Nailsea Lass* pushed steadily north at her best speed of 6 knots. On the 16th, when abeam of the Straits of Gibraltar, she made her first contact with the rest of the world when a patrolling British warship intercepted her, but made off at speed after a brief exchange of signals. A few hours later, the *Nailsea Lass* ran into a strong head gale and was soon burying her bows into an angry sea, her speed reduced to no more than 3 knots. To her crew it seemed like the all too familiar welcome home to northern waters. Eight days later, on the evening of the 24th, the *Nailsea Lass* was 60 miles to the southwest of the Fasnet Rock and heading up the Irish coast towards the North Channel, wartime gateway to the British ports. The weather was fine, with good visibility and only a light wind and a low swell to disturb the surface of the sea. The first stirrings of spring could be sensed in the air but the night was cold.

At fifteen minutes before eight o'clock, Chief Officer Alfred Hodder paced the wing of the bridge feeling more than content with his lot. The last minutes of the watch were ticking away, one of the few remaining watches he would have to stand in this passage, which had already stretched to twenty-six gruelling days. The threat of the enemy, too, was receeding for, very soon, the *Nailsea Lass* would come under the protection of the warships and aircraft guarding the Western Approaches. In a few days, if no unforeseen disaster occurred, she would be safe in port and all the tensions and fears of the long, lonely passage would disperse as the fog does under the touch of a warm sun.

Hodder's dream of the other world was rudely shattered when the *Nailsea Lass* staggered under the blow of a giant sledgehammer. Seconds later, the explosion came like a clap of thunder. Momentarily deafened, Hodder watched a huge column of water erupt from port side of the ship, abreast the forward masthouse. As the column toppled and the sea began to rain down on the bridge, he dived for the engineroom telegraph and swung the handle to the stop position. The wounded ship vibrated roughly as her engine slowed abruptly and ground to a halt. She began to list ominously to port as the water poured into her holds.

When the torpedo struck, Second Officer Ernest Knight was in his cabin below the bridge preparing to turn in. As is the lot of most second officers in merchant ships, he had the punishing middle watch, midnight to 04.00, which guaranteed him a night of broken sleep every night while the ship was at sea. When the *Nailsea Lass* reeled over to starboard and the explosion came, Knight was at once aware that, on this night, there would be no need for him to go through the usual routine of courting sleep while the rest of the ship was awake. As he lunged for his lifejacket, he heard from the bridge the urgent voice of Captain Bradford give the order to abandon ship. Knight's next movements, rehearsed in his mind so many times, were almost automatic. Taking the bridge ladder at a rush, he hurried into the dimly-lit chartroom and began to bundle the ship's secret code and signal books into the weighted bag kept handy. As he was so engaged, he felt the ship settling by the bow and lost no time in tumbling out onto the deck. He ran to the rail and hurled the Admiralty's secrets into the dark sea below. His primary duty done, he looked to himself.

Reaching the boat deck, Knight was surprised to learn there had been no casualties, in spite of the fact that, in the style of her day, the *Nailsea Lass* housed her ratings under her forecastle head, not 40 feet forward of where she had been hit. The weather was still in a kindly mood and the ship was abandoned in an orderly fashion, all 36 men getting away in the two lifeboats. It was fortunate they wasted no time for, as they pulled clear, the stern of their ship rose high in the air and she slid under, bow first. The chartroom clock showed exactly 20.00 as the water closed over it. But there would be no change of the watch in the *Nailsea Lass*, this night or ever again.

As the Welsh seamen lay back on their oars, silently mourning the loss of their ship, Kapitän-Leutnant Herbert Schultze took one last precautionary look through his periscope and gave the order to blow tanks. Second Officer Knight, at the tiller of the Captain's boat, sucked in his breath as *U-48*, her black hull cascading water, surfaced close by and immediately motored over to the Chief Officer's boat. The U-boat commander appeared in the conning tower and Knight heard him, in good English, order Hodder to bring his boat alongside. The Chief Officer obeyed, and, after a short exchange with the commander, boarded the submarine and disappeared below. Being well aware of the German Navy's policy of pulling senior merchant ship officers out of circulation, Knight knew he was unlikely to see Hodder again until after the war.

It was Captain Bradford's turn next for, with a flurry of white water at her stern, the U-boat was now approaching his boat. Rising and falling on the low swell, the boat bumped heavily on the casing of the submarine as she came alongside. As Knight ordered his crew to fend off, his eyes met Bradford's and an unspoken farewell passed between them.

The lifeboat drifted astern until it was abreast of the conning tower and Knight looked up to see a tall figure in a white-topped cap, Herbert Schultze, leaning over the rail. Schultze first inquired if there were any injured in the boat then, in a conversation with Bradford, who made no attempt to conceal his rank, expressed his regret at having had to sink the *Nailsea Lass*. Nevertheless, he then took the Captain prisoner and the U-boat made off on the surface at speed.

With Bradford and Hodder having been whisked away into captivity, Knight was now in command of the survivors of the *Nailsea Lass*. He immediately closed the other lifeboat, now in the charge of the nineteen year-old Third Officer Gouge, to discuss their plight. He discovered Schultze had given Gouge two packets of cigarettes and a course for the nearest land – a poor exchange for the ship's two senior men. While the cigarettes were appreciated the course was of little use to the Third Officer, for his compass had been damaged in the torpedoing. Knight was now faced with the decision to either lash the two boats together and remain in the vicinity of the sinking awaiting rescue, or to set course for the land. The prospect of an early search being made for them was extremely unlikely, as the *Nailsea Lass*'s transmitter had been smashed by the explosion and no SOS had been sent out before she sank. Knight decided to make for the Irish coast, a little over 60 miles to the northeast. There was insufficient wind for sailing so the two boats set off rowing in close company.

At midnight the wind began to freshen from the southwest and, with hopes of an early landing rising, Knight ordered the sails to be hoisted and they ran free before the wind. During the course of the night, the two boats became separated but Knight decided to press on alone and, by late afternoon on the 25th, had the land in sight. As darkness was now closing in and the wind and sea rising, Knight elected to heave to and wait for daylight before approaching the rocky coast. Further south, Gouge had arrived at the same decision. Tragedy now began to stalk the men of the *Nailsea Lass*, who had survived the assaults of the enemy. A depression moving quickly in from the Atlantic brought a howling gale which, accompanied by driving rain, added to the vile discomfort of the bitterly cold night. Before morning came, five men, three firemen, an ordinary seaman and the cook had died of exposure in the half-swamped lifeboats. For them, it was a cold and miserable death, a cruel ending to a long voyage which had climaxed in the loss of their ship, their belongings and their dignity.

Although the *Nailsea Lass* was long gone under 70 fathoms of grey Atlantic water, with five of her men now dead and two in captivity, her survivors continued the fight to live and sail again. Knight succeeded in bringing his boat in through the Blasket Sound to land at Ballyoughtraugh, Co. Kerry, on the morning of the 26th. A few hours later, nineteen year-old Gouge, who had seen four men die in his boat during the night, gained the shelter of Bantry Bay and made the shore at Bearhaven. It was a day short of a month since they had sailed from Freetown in the company of Convoy SLS 64.

A jubilant Herbert Schultze brought *U-48* into Brest eleven days later, where he was duly presented with the Ritter Kreuz by Konter-Admiral Dönitz, C-in-C Submarines. Before the end of March, *U-48* and Schultze returned to sea to sink another 49,363 tons of Allied shipping, before the submarine was taken out of service in the summer of that year. Herbert Schultze survived the war with the rank of Kapitän-zur-See. He still lives. *U-48* came to an ignominious end, being scuttled in a North German port ahead of the Allied advance in May 1945.

12

The St Patrick: death in the
St George's Channel

Following the unexpected capitulation of France in June 1940, Germany gained control of an additional 800 miles of Atlantic coastline, stretching from the Dover Strait to Northern Spain. This was a catastrophic blow to the hard-pressed Royal Navy. The scratching of the pens on the surrender document in that historic railway carriage in the forest of Compiegne, in effect, moved the U-boats 1,000 miles nearer to their hunting grounds off the west coast of Ireland. Relocated in the Biscay ports of Brest, Lorient, St Nazaire and Bordeaux, they had access to the whole of the Atlantic with reduced risk of attack on passage and an immense saving in time and fuel on their voyaging to and from the convoy lanes.

The Admiralty quickly offset some of this advantage by laying an extensive minefield in the Western Approaches, effectively sealing off both the St George's Channel and the English Channel from the south and west. All shipping bound for British ports was then routed further north, in through the North Channel between Scotland and Northern Ireland, or around the north of Scotland if bound for East Coast ports. The time during which the Atlantic convoys were vunerable to attack by U-boats was thus considerably shortened.

One ship to gain particular benefit from this isolation of the St George's Channel behind the minefield was the 1,922-ton cross-channel steamer *St Patrick*, which had hitherto been making the 54-mile passage between Fishguard Harbour and Rosslare under constant threat of U-boat attack. Owned by the Fishguard & Rosslare Railways and Harbours Company and commanded by Captain James Faraday, the *St Patrick* kept open a tenuous but vital link between Britain and neutral Eire, carrying passengers and cargo. To a man, her crew was drawn from the twin towns of Fishguard and Goodwick.

Although the St George's Channel was made safe from the attentions of the U-boats, it was still open to the long range Focke-Wulf Condors and JU-88's of the Luftwaffe based at Stavanger and Bordeaux. The *St Patrick* had been bombed and machine gunned by one of these aircraft in August 1940 but had escaped without serious damage or casualties. The guardian angel of this little ship seemed a zealous one. One of the key members of the *St Patrick*'s crew was Stewardess Agnes Swayne, who watched over the women passengers in Second Class. At forty-five, prematurely greyed by the hard knocks life had dealt her, Agnes was a strong, capable woman, whose eyes were tinged with a deep sadness. Widowed at thirty, with five small children to rear in a world uncushioned by welfare payments, she had struggled alone for eight years, always short of money but fired by love and determination. The offer of a post as stewardess in the cross-channel steamers had been a small miracle. With a steady income and her children growing to maturity, she was at last able to look forward to a life offering contentment and a degree of security. And so it was for seven more years until, in the early hours of the morning of 2 December 1940, some 400 miles west of Bloody Foreland, Kapitän-Leutnant Ernst Mengersen turned his sights on the *Lady Glanely*. For Agnes Swayne the old, half-forgotten agony of fourteen years ago came flooding back, this time with a cruel twist. Although her son Oswald, junior engineer in the *Lady Glanely* was posted as missing, presumed lost at sea, there was no confirmation of his death. Soon after, rumours circulating that the survivors of the *Lady Glanely* had been taken prisoner by the U-boat offered her a straw at which she was to clutch for six long months.

Seafaring is a hazardous calling and it is not surprising those who follow it are superstitious by nature. Friday, because of its associations with the Crucifixtion, has always been thought to be an unlucky day on which to set sail. Should that Friday happen to be on the Thirteenth day of the month, it is considered by seamen to be doubly inauspicious. Even in this present age of hard-nosed reality, shipmasters are still known to shun Friday the Thirteenth and will often deliberately avoid sailing on that day.

As master of a cross-channel steamer committed to a tight schedule, Captain James Faraday was unable to allow himself the luxury of indulging in such unprofessional manipulation. Shortly before one o'clock on the morning of Friday 13 June 1941, the *St Patrick*, having embarked her passengers and cargo, left her berth in Rosslare harbour. Weather permitting – and the report was favourable – Faraday was confident of arriving in Fishguard in ample time to connect with the London boat train at 06.00.

The weather was fine and clear, with only a light wind blowing, as the *St Patrick* left the lights of Rosslare astern. On the bridge, Captain Faraday looked forward to a quiet crossing of the St George's Channel. The minefield in the south and the Navy's anti-submarine patrols in the north had made this fifty-four mile-wide stretch of water as safe as it could be. There was still, of course the danger of attack by enemy aircraft, as the ship had encountered some ten months earlier, but the possibility of lightning striking twice in the same place seemed most unlikely to Faraday. His ship was fast and the crossing short. Not long after sunrise she would be inside the breakwaters of Fishguard Harbour and safe under the towering cliffs of Pen Cw. The port formalities would be as brief as usual and Faraday looked forward with pleasure to the brisk morning walk from the harbour to his house on the outskirts of Goodwick. And he would not be alone as he strode up the harbour road on this fine summer's morning. Accompanying him as a passenger on this voyage was his twenty year-old son Jack, a Merchant Navy cadet on leave from his own ship. Of Faraday's three sons, all serving their country, Jack was the only one to adopt his father's chosen career, and therefore held a special place in the Captain's heart.

In the *St Patrick*'s accommodation, Stewardesses Jane Hughes and May Owen had settled in their women charges among the forty-four passengers soon after sailing and, with the weather in an obviously benevolent mood, they too were expecting a quiet passage. Although their port duties would not allow them to leave the ship as early as Captain Faraday, the two stewardesses were also looking forward to spending a few hours with their families in Goodwick. For May Owen, this was an extra trip, having volunteered to stand in for Agnes Swayne who, after so many tortured months of waiting, had at last received official confirmation of the death of her son Oswald in the sinking of the *Lady Glanely*. Agnes, worn down by the prolonged uncertainty, had been unable to face the ordeal of supervising passengers with a false smile on her lips.

At 04.26 on the morning of the 13th, the *St Patrick* was 10 miles off Strumble Head, the frowning northwestern headland of Pencaer, and slicing her way through the water towards Fishguard Harbour, fourteen miles to to southeast. The sun was just twenty minutes below the horizon, its first rays already fingering the clear sky. The usual early morning onshore breeze had arisen, kicking up whitecaps on the still-dark surface of the sea, but they did nothing to impede the progress of *St Patrick* on the last few miles of her passage. Pacing the bridge, Captain Faraday was experiencing the satisfaction of another voyage completed on time and without incident. Below in the accommodation, a few restless passengers stirred but the majority slept on while Jane Hughes and May Owen quietly prepared for the coming disembarkation.

There was no prior warning of the attack. The German aircraft came in from the dark side, unseen by the bridge lookouts or the men manning the 12-pounder gun on the dawn stand-by. Either by luck or uncanny judgement, the stick of four bombs landed squarely on the cross-bunker fuel tanks, which ran the breadth of the ship immediately forward of her funnel. The *St Patrick* erupted in a ball of fire and began to sink at once.

The massive explosion wiped out the First Class accommodation on the boat deck, killing all its occupants except one.
Stewardess Jane Hughes died with them. Ironically, the less
privileged passengers below decks fared better, although they
suffered a frightening ordeal. They found themselves in complete darkness, with the ship listing heavily and overall the
cloying stench of fuel oil escaping from the ruptured bunker
tanks. As the living tried to grope their way through the maze
of unfamiliar allyways and ladders, the crackle of flames added
to their fears. A group of frightened women in the lowest deck
seemed doomed to go down with the ship until May Owen,
with complete disregard for her own life, fought her way
through the chaos and led them to safety on deck.

It was fortunate that, on this occasion, the *St Patrick*'s crew
outnumbered her passengers by 45 to 44, for within seven
minutes of being hit the ship was on her way down. Captain
Faraday's men, and one remaining woman, acted with magnificent courage and cool efficiency. It was possible to launch
only one of the ship's lifeboats, this being quickly dropped
to the water manned by two seamen. Those passengers who
had survived the bombing had to be coaxed into the water,
some requiring considerable persuasion, for the wind had risen
further and the sea was developing an angry chop. The lifeboat,
manned by Steward George Walters and another crew
member, plucked 30 survivors from the water while other seamen swam around dragging the luckless passengers onto liferafts. Many of them covered with black oil, which was escaping
from the *St Patrick*'s tanks and adding further agony to the
tragedy at sunrise.

Stewardess May Owen refused to leave the ship until she
had seen all her women passengers into their lifejackets and
over the side. She was about to leave herself when she heard
the cries of another woman still below decks. Although she
realized the ship had only a few minutes to live, May Owen
went below again, brought the woman up on deck and jumped
over the side with her. Neither woman had a lifejacket and,
for the next two hours, the stewardess supported the passenger

in the rough, oil-covered sea, until they were both pulled onto a raft.

Second Engineer Frank Purcell, who had already saved three of his men trapped in the engineroom after the bombing, also rescued a wounded fellow crew member and kept him afloat until they reached the safety of a liferaft. Young Jack Faraday, a strong swimmer, had no difficulty in getting away from the sinking ship. It would have been easy for him to join the others on the rafts, but, when he discovered his father was missing, he swam back towards the blazing wreck. He was never seen again.

At 04.33 on the morning of Friday 13 June, as the rays of the rising sun were striking fire from the summit of Mynydd Preseli, to the east of Fishguard Bay, the *St Patrick* slipped below the waves with a fierce hissing of quenched fires. Sixty-five men, women and children were left to fight for their lives against a hostile, rising sea.

There was a noticeable air of unease in the twin towns of Fishguard and Goodwick on that Friday morning. Fears were not only expressed but many an anxious eye was turned upon the empty ferry terminal as the towns went about their morning's work. The school children of Goodwick, making their morning trek to the County Grammar School in Fishguard, were unusually subdued as they hurried along the open road fronting the bay. The ship in which many of their fathers served should have been at her accustomed berth for more than two hours. Where was she? Somehow, the children sensed the pleasant order of their young lives was about to be roughly disturbed. The tense situation in the towns was heightened when, in a flurry of spray, the Fishguard lifeboat, *Whitestar*, roared down its slipway and headed out through the breakwaters at full speed. Word was passed around that an unidentified ship was of fire off Strumble Head.

Circling to the northwest of Strumble head, the lifeboat found an ominous patch of oil on the water, a few pieces of unidentifiable wreckage but no survivors. Stopping only to pick up two fish boxes seen floating in the vicinity of the oilslick, the lifeboat headed back to the harbour, concluding that some unfortunate fishing boat had foundered, taking all hands with it. It was only when the lifeboat was back in harbour that the fears of those on shore began to move towards awful reality. The fish boxes brought back were identified by their markings as being from the *St Patrick*'s cargo. The lifeboat returned to sea at once to resume her search, but it was now apparent to all involved that a terrible calamity was about to envelop the towns.

Within the walls of the County School the sounds of laughter were stilled as ashen-faced teachers gently took aside and sent home those pupils whose fathers were known to have been on board the *St Patrick*. It seemed their mothers would soon need the comfort of their presence. If there is a special god who watches over seamen, then he must surely have been in the vicinity of Strumble Head on that June morning in 1941. When the *St Patrick* sank, seven minutes after being hit by the stick of bombs, she left behind her 65 survivors. Thirty were crammed into one lifeboat, while the rest were on or clinging to liferafts, which were constantly being capsized by the rough sea. Many of them were covered in fuel oil, all were cold, wretched and frightened. Those who knew took comfort from the fact that the *St Patrick*'s wireless operator had been able to get away an SOS before she sank. Also the ship had been burning and within sight of Strumble Head lighthouse, when she went down. Rescue, in the form of the Fishguard lifeboat, stationed only fourteen miles away, must surely already be on the way. An hour passed, and then two, but there was still no sign of the familiar blue and white painted craft rounding the headland of Pen Anglas.

It seems likely that had these wretched people been condemned to await the arrival of the Fishguard lifeboat, many of them would have died. As luck or that special seamen's god – would have it, a convoy was passing off the coast at the time of the sinking and the *St Patrick*'s cry for help was answered by the naval escorts. Just over two hours after they had been so cruelly cast into the sea, the 65 survivors were picked up. Three hours later they were landed at Milford Haven and word was flashed to Fishguard Harbour. For the people of Fishguard and Goodwick, the news of the rescue brought blessed relief but there could be little rejoicing. It was though a dark, funeral cloud had drifted in over Fishguard Bay. Never again would the little *St Patrick* be seen trailing her plume of smoke through the breakwaters. Captain James Faraday would walk the harbour road no more, neither would his gallant son Jack. Jane Hughes was dead and so were fifteen men of the towns. Friday 13 June 1941, which brought grief to many, widowhood to some and made orphans of the innocent, would be remembered with horror for a long, long time.

To Agnes Swayne, who should have been at the side of Jane Hughes that morning, it was clear she had been spared by the sacrifice of her son on a dark December night in the North Atlantic. It was a life for a life.

On a grey afternoon in November 1982, the Sealink ferry *Stena Normandica* lay hove to ten miles to the northwest of Strumble Head, whose white-painted lighthouse dominates the peninsula of Pencaer. With only the melancholy cries of the wheeling gulls as an accompaniment, a brief service was held and a wreath of flowers laid on the water in remembrance of those who had lost their lives in the *St Patrick* forty-one years before. It was a sad reflection on the state of Britain's Merchant Navy that the flag at the dip at the ferry's stern was not the red Ensign but the blue and yellow of Sweden. How the ghosts of those who died for their country within sight of its rocky shores must have wept on that day – not for their lost years but for a maritime heritage that was no more.

13

The Llanover: America lends a hand

The bombing of Pearl Harbour by the Japanese in December 1941 finally brought a hitherto reluctant United States of America into the war. Within a few days, Admiral Dönitz, always alert to new opportunities, moved a small force of his U-boats into the far-Western Atlantic. The US Navy woefully inexperienced in anti-submarine warfare, found itself easily outwitted by these savage marauders. Operating close into the American sea-board, from New York to the Caribbean, the Germans sank over 100 ships of 750,000 tons in the first four months of 1942. Only one U-boat was lost.

The campaign gave birth to a new crop of U-boat aces, among them Korvetten-Kapitän Johann Mohr, who commanded *U-124*. Unfortunately for Mohr and his fellow submariners, the Americans quickly brought their defences into order and the U-boats were forced to retire to the less inhospitable waters of mid-Atlantic. By the end of April, Mohr, with nine sinkings to his credit, was to be found haunting the northern convoy route in the vicinity of 29 degrees West. He was accompanied by Kapitän-Leutnant Hans-Peter Hinsch in *U-569* and Kapitän-Leutnant Otto Ites in *U-94*.

Eight hundred miles to the east of the trio's search area lay the island of Islay, in the Inner Hebrides. Islay boasts one of the only Celtic churches in Scotland, a host of distilleries and a climate ranging from miserable to malignant, for there is nothing but 2,000 miles of uninterrupted Atlantic Ocean to the west of the island. Loch Indaal, a deep bay-like fiord, which all but cuts Islay in two, provides the only shelter from the restless ocean.

On the morning of 7 May 1942, the tiny, whitewashed cottages clinging to the hillsides overlooking Loch Indaal witnessed the assembling of Convoy ONS 92. By noon that day, a total of forty-one merchant ships, most of them riding light, had gathered in the grey waters of the loch. Two hours later, the merchantmen were joined by their escorts for the coming voyage, a combined force of US and Canadian naval ships, which had earlier set out from Lough Foyle on the other side of the North Channel. Flags raced up the halyards, signal lamps winked and, within an hour, Convoy ONS 92 was steaming purposefully westwards towards the granaries and arsenals of North America.

Occupying an uncomfortably exposed position in the middle of the port outer column of ONS 92 was the steamer *Llanover*, owned by Evan Thomas, Radcliffe & Co., of Cardiff and commanded by Captain Lionel Osborne. The 4,979-ton *Llanover*, Sunderland built in 1928, was as undistinguished as a tramp of her day could be, with a bow as straight as a West Wales cliff face, counter stern, accommodation in square blocks and a tall 'Woodbine' funnel providing natural draught for her economy-conscious Scotch boilers. She would break no records for miles steamed per day, nor would her spartan accommodation raise shouts of acclaim, but she was a sound, reliable ship, well crewed and ably commanded.

Although Captain Osborne was perhaps uneasy about his vunerable position in the convoy – he would be one of the first in the U-boat's sights in the event of an attack – he did have cause to look forward to the Atlantic crossing with some confidence. ONS 92 was a slow convoy – not more than $7\frac{1}{2}$ knots – and suited the limited capability of the *Llanover*'s engines; it also had in the combined North American force, a powerful escort. Moreover, the weather was good and, being early summer, looked set to stay that way. For all that, the passage would be no week-end pleasure cruise for Osborne and his crew. Two weeks of continuous tension and sleepless nights would take their toll. At the end of it there was, admittedly, the compensation of a short break in a land as yet untroubled by the hardships of war, but in the background there would always be the prospect of the homeward passage, deep loaded and doubly at risk.

For Johann Mohr, Hans-Peter Hinsch and Otto Ites the waiting had been long. At dawn on 11 May they were still cruising idly in the region of latitude 53 degrees North, longitude 29 degrees West, the mid-point of the convoy route across the North Atlantic. The weather continued fine, with a light Easterly wind, smooth sea and good visibility. Later that morning, the trio's patience was rewarded by the sight of smoke curling up from the eastern horizon. First one, then two, then a forest of masts and funnels came into view, silhouetted by the rising sun. Convoy ONS 92, apparently unaware of the danger, was steaming straight into their trap. The U-boats submerged and prepared for the familiar game of cat and mouse, shadowing the convoy by day and racing in to attack under the cover of darkness.

But before submerging, Mohr and his companions gave themselves away by engaging in needless radio chatter. An alert wireless operator on the convoy's rescue ship, the British steamer *Bury* picked up their transmissions and reported to the convoy escort commander. Later in the day, the *Bury*'s report was confirmed by the Admiralty Submarine Tracking Room in London, which had intercepted and decoded positional messages from the U-boats to BdU in Lorient. It was a common failing with the U-boats that they found it difficult, or thought it unnecessary to keep radio silence when they were in the Atlantic. For many of them it had been their downfall.

Shortly after receipt of the Admiralty's warning, the convoy escort commander, in USS *Gleaves*, took his ship, in company with USS *Spencer*, and made a visual and asdic search right around the convoy up to a distance of eighteen miles. At ten minutes before six, with the sun low in the west, *Gleaves* sighted a U-boat on the surface and gave chase. The pursuit was futile for, as soon as the American ship came within gun range, the U-boat submerged. *Gleaves* continued to search with asdic and twice made contact with the U-boat but was unable to sink her. The hunt went on after dark, with *Gleaves* and *Spencer* making broad sweeps around the convoy which, with all ships in a state of constant readiness, continued to zig-zag towards the west.

On board the *Llanover* the atmosphere was electric. Warned of the presence of U-boats by a general signal made by the convoy commodore, Osborne had made what preparations he could to meet the expected attack. Lifejackets were donned, all guns manned and lookouts doubled. The night, when it came, was fine and clear; perfect weather for the U-boats to do their work. Osborne was now, more than ever, acutely aware of his ship's exposed position. His fears increased when at 23.00, just as the convoy had discontinued zig-zagging, two rockets soared into the air from a ship ahead of the *Llanover* and burst in a flurry of brilliant white stars. *U-124* had opened the action.

Ringing the alarm bells was something of an irrelevancy but Osborne did it nevertheless, bringing his already alert crew into a fine pitch of readiness. He swung his binoculars in the direction of the commodore's ship, expecting the coloured lights to flare indicating an emergency turn, which normally followed the torpedoing of a ship in convoy. The commodore's ship remained in darkness. Five minutes later, the *Llanover* had drawn abeam of the torpedoed ship, which Osborne identified as the leader of his column, the 7,065-ton *Empire Dell*.

As Osborne was silently debating the advisibility of going to the aid of the sinking ship, the lookout on the port wing of the *Llanover* shouted a warning. Swinging around, Osborne was in time to see the phosphorescent track of a torpedo speeding towards his ship from three points abaft the beam. Johann Mohr had fired his second arrow. It was too late for Osborne to take evasive action. At the *Llanover*'s speed of $7\frac{1}{2}$ knots, even with the wheel hard over it would be several minutes before she would begin to cant. The torpedo took her in the port quarter, squarely in her after cargo hold. The force of the explosion ripped open the half-inch steel plates of the ship's side as though they were so much parchment, and the Atlantic poured into the empty hold.

The *Llanover* lurched drunkenly to port and the steady beat of her engines suddenly accelerated to a frantic tattoo, before slowing to a shuddering halt as the main steam valve was spun shut. The explosion in the after hold had demolished the propellor shaft tunnel, which ran the length of the hold, snapping the hardened steel shaft like a brittle stick. The *Llanover* was now a ship without means of propulsion. Sadly, Osborne walked over to the big brass engineroom telegraph and swung the handle to 'Finished with Engines' for the last time. He prayed the watertight door giving access from the engineroom to the shaft tunnel had been lowered into the closed position as soon as the alarm bells had sounded. As if to protest at the deep wound she had suffered, the *Llanover*'s steam whistle now added its voice to the confusion, filling the night with a high pitched wail of anguish. All efforts to silence it were unsuccessful, some buckling of the funnel having jammed the steam valve in the open position. Shouting above the din, Osborne ordered his Third Officer to launch the two rockets whose white stars would alert the rest of the convoy to their plight. One of the rockets blew up when it was ignited, severely scorching the junior officer's hand.

The *Llanover* was settling quickly by the stern and Osborne was not surprised to learn that the watertight door between the engineroom and the shaft tunnel had been open when the torpedo struck. The engineroom was flooding and had been evacuated. The situation moved from serious to desperate but Osborne, with the ingrained loyalty of a master mariner, was reluctant to let go of his ship. He believed she might still be saved but he was also aware that the U-boat might at any moment put a second torpedo into her. His immediate, overriding concern was therefore to save the lives of his crew. He gave the order to abandon ship. The two lifeboats were lowered without mishap and Osborne and his men left the ship unhurriedly and without panic. Miraculously, the only casualty of the attack was the Third Officer, whose hand had been burned by the exploding rocket.

Once clear of the ship, Osborne was for the first time able to survey the damage. The whole of the *Llanover*'s poop structure had been demolished and she was visibly down by the stern. With her propellor shaft gone, she would be unable to steam under her own power, but there was always the possibility of a tow. As the sea was reasonably calm, Osborne decided to wait out the night in the boats and attempt to reboard the ship next morning, assuming she was still afloat. However, an hour later the convoy rescue ship *Bury* arrived on the scene and Osborne, much as he hated leaving his stricken ship could not refuse his men the chance of safety.

Following the sinking of the *Empire Dell* and the attack on the *Llanover* by *U-124*, ONS 92 appears to have continued steaming without taking any violent evasive action. This gave the other U-boats the opportunity to move in quickly. Hinsch, in *U-569*, fired first and, although he claimed a hit, his fan of torpedoes passed harmlessly through the lines of the convoy. Ites in *U-94* had better luck, sinking the 5,630-ton Panama-flag ship *Cocle* shortly after midnight. Fifteen minutes later, Mohr returned to the attack, sinking in quick succession the 4,371-ton Greek ship *Mount Parnes* and the 5,389-ton British steamer *Cristales*. It was only then the commodore ordered a series of emergency turns. These manoeuvres, combined with intense escort activity, forced the U-boats to withdraw. Signals heard on 500 Kcs during the night indicated the Germans were still in the vicinity but they took no further action against the convoy.

At dawn the *Llanover* was still afloat and in sight from the deck of the rescue ship. Captain Osborne immediately requested permission to return to his ship with a skeleton crew. The escort commander, no doubt understanding Osborne's feelings for his ship, agreed to a reboarding, with the proviso that the *Llanover* was able to proceed under her own steam. Osborne was unable to give such a guarantee, knowing in his heart that his ship would never steam again. He did, how-ever, persuade the master of the *Bury* to turn back and close the *Llanover*. As they drew near, it became clear that the torpe-doed ship was slowly sinking and Osborne was forced to con-cede defeat. Three hours later, he watched grim-faced as the Canadian corvette *Arvida* administered the coup de grace with her guns. The *Llanover* went down at 09.46, almost eleven hours after being hit.

The night of the 12th was again fine and clear, with a smooth sea. The U-boats returned soon after dark and were sighted from time to time on the surface stalking the convoy like the shadowy wolves they were. The American destroyers *Gleaves* and *Spencer* raced into the attack with guns and depth charges whenever the opportunity arose, and with apparent good effect. Mohr and the luckless Hinsch were driven off. Ites, however, was able to evade the escorts and, at 00.22 on the 13th, as the convoy was in the process of completing a pre-arranged 90 degree turn to port, *U-94* sank the 4,399-ton British ship *Batna* and, four hours later the Swedish *Tolken* of 4,471 tons.

The convoy was not further molested but, it must be said that two of the three U-boats involved had achieved consider-able success. Between them they had sunk 7 ships, totalling 36,284 tons. Of the handling of Convoy ONS 92 during the forty-eight hours it was under attack, some doubts must be raised. The presence of the U-boats was detected early on the morning of the 11th, some eighteen hours before the first torpedoing. No less than three messages were received from the Admiralty during that day, warning that the convoy was being shadowed and its position being reported to Lorient by one or more enemy submarines. Yet, apart from zig-zagging about the mean course, the convoy appears to have taken no positive evasive action throughout the day and much of the following night. It was not until the fifth ship had been sunk, at around 01.00 on the 12th, that the commodore instituted a sucession of emergency turns designed to spoil the aim of the U-boats, who were already among the convoy. It is feasible that, had ONS 92 made a radical alteration of course as soon as complete darkness came on the night of the 11th and run away from the U-boats, there would have been no sinkings. Of course, it is no mean feat of collective seamanship to put forty-one merchant ships, sailing in close order, through a radical change of course at night without using lights. However, this manoeuvre had been successfully used in convoys escorted by the Royal Navy for some time. It may be that the relatively inexperienced American escort commander of ONS 92, like many of his compatriots prefered to perfect his own methods of anti-submarine warfare, rather than adopt the well-tried British tactics.

On the afternoon of 13 May, the *Bury*, which now had 143 survivors on board and was running short of food, was ordered to leave the convoy and head for St John's Newfoundland, some 700 miles away. With her went Captain Osborne and the men of the *Llanover*. They had lost their ship but, before many weeks had elapsed, they would be back at sea, in a new ship, and carrying on with what to them was just a job of work.

Johann Mohr and his two companions remained in the area after the passing of ONS 92, no doubt encouraged by their success. Less than a month later, they were able to set up a similar ambush for Convoy ONS 100 as it sailed westward in the track of ONS 92. Once again Hinsch failed to score a hit, but Mohr and Ites between them disposed of five ships, including the 4,458-ton *Pontypridd*, owned by Morel Ltd, of Cardiff.

U-124 went on to sink another 44,443 tons of Allied shipping before being destroyed off Oporto on 2 April 1943 by the Royal Australian Navy sloop *Swan* and the British corvette *Stonecrop*. Korvetten-Kapitän Johann Mohr perished with his crew.

14

The Garlinge: operation torch

Whan William Barnes of Aberaman assumed command of the 2,012-ton *Garlinge* at Greenock in October 1942, he took upon his shoulders a task men twice his age might have shunned. Barnes was serving as chief officer in the ship when the exigencies of war, in the form of a mounting casualty list of senior officers prompted his sudden promotion to command. He was then twenty-six years old, with the ink barely dry on his master's certificate. The *Garlinge*, on the other hand, was reaching the geriatric stage of her life.

Built in 1918, when an earlier world war was just drawing to a close, the *Garlinge* was one of an original fleet of seven owned by Constants (South Wales) Ltd of Cardiff, whose trade was between British and the Mediterranean ports. She was a small, conventional steamship, 284 feet long, 42 feet in the beam and, in her younger days, had been capable of a top speed of 10 knots. Three of her sisters had already been lost by enemy action in this present war and, as the newly-promoted Captain Barnes was all too well aware, the *Garlinge* might soon become the fourth casualty. Their Lordships, in their wisdom had chosen her to take part in the first great amphibious invasion of the war. For a ship of her size and doubtful capability, the risks involved in her forthcoming voyage would be enormous.

Operation 'Torch' was to be an assault on the North African ports of Casablanca, Algiers and Oran, using American and Canadian troops carried in British ships. In the first landings, 90,000 men and their equipment were scheduled to be put

s/s *Garlinge* 2021 GRT. Sunk by *U-81* in Mediterranean 10 November 1942 while taking part in the Allied invasion of North Africa.

ashore at the three beachheads. The total fleet, including escorts, was to number 340 ships, one section sailing across the Atlantic with the American contingent and the other to carry the First Canadian Division from Britain. Meticulous planning called for all the ships to pass through – in the case of Casablanca bound ships, close to – the Straits of Gibraltar between the night of the 5th and the morning of 7 November. The landings were to take place simultaneously on the morning of the 8th.

German intelligence was aware an Allied invasion of North Africa was about to take place – this had already been leaked by Free French and Russian sources – but they had been unable to discover the precise location of the assault. Hitler favoured Dakar and ordered a force of forty U-boats to patrol the approaches to Northwest Africa, between Gibraltar and Senegal. In the western Mediterranean, a smaller combined force of German and Italian U-boats was operating off North Africa as part of the normal offensive against Allied shipping. Among these modern corsairs of the Barbary Coast was Kapitän-Leutnant Friedrich Guggenberger in *U-81*. Guggenberger was no stranger to this area, having torpedoed and sunk the 22,600-ton British carrier *Ark Royal* near Gibraltar twelve months earlier.

When the *Garlinge* left the Clyde on 21 October, although she was to be an integral part of Operation Torch, her cargo of 2,700 tons of coal seemed singularly unwarlike for the operation in which she was engaged. It was as though she was considered too old and slow to be trusted with anything more than the cargo she carried outwards from South Wales for so much of her life before the war. But to young Captain Barnes and his crew their ship's role in the coming invasion was as vital as that of any of the bigger ships carrying troops and guns. In the sandy plains of North Africa, their cargo would be very much in demand after the first flush of battle. Coal was a source of energy without which no invasion force of the day could survive for long.

The eight-day passage from the Clyde to Gibraltar passed without serious incident, giving Barnes a much needed breathing space to settle in to his new command. He was fortunate to have with him as chief officer Robert Macmillan, a man of nearly thirty years his senior. The youth of Barnes and the wisdom and experience of Macmillan provided a good basis for a happy and efficient ship at a time when the war at sea was reaching another peak. In the previous month no less than 87 Allied merchant ships had been sunk by U-boats in the Atlantic. The 1,400 mile passage south to Gibraltar would require strong nerves and expert judgement.

In the closing days of October, when the invasion fleets were nearing the approaches to the Mediterranean, the patrolling U-boats were by chance drawn away to the south by the sighting of Convoy SL 125, homeward bound in ballast from Freetown. In a running battle that lasted four days and ranged from the Canaries to a position 500 miles to the west of Gibraltar, SL 125 lost 13 ships, but its sacrifices undoubtedly saved the heavily laden invasion fleets. While the men of SL 125 were fighting for their lives, the great armada of ships carrying the wherewithall to mount Operation Torch slipped past undetected. In their midst was the small, unassuming Welsh collier *Garlinge*.

After a short stop in Gibraltar, the *Garlinge* left that port on the night of 7 November in the rear of the main invasion fleet, which had already sailed for Algiers. In company with her were three other merchant ships and an escort of five anti-submarine trawlers. The four merchantmen set off in line abreast, with the escorting trawlers positioned ahead, astern and on either beam of the small convoy. There was none of the bustling majesty of a great Atlantic convoy, attended by destroyers and corvettes, all anxious to show off their bow waves. However, Barnes was reasonably happy with the arrangement. Five escorts to four merchant ships was very reassuring, even if the escorts were only old fishermen dressed up to look like men of war. Furthermore, the *Garlinge* should be able to give as good as she got if attacked. She mounted a 12-pounder, four 20 mm Oerlikons capable of firing 500 rounds a minute, two twin-Marlin machine guns and the usual array of anti-aircraft rockets. These guns were not manned by enthusiastic seamen with only a passing knowledge of gunnery but by a trained force of 13 Naval and Army gunners. Barnes, was of course, assuming the attack, if and when it came, would be from the air. The first threat, in fact, came from a neutral source.

It had long been an accepted myth, perpetuated by poets and, more lately travel agents, that the Mediterranean Sea is placid, blue lake undisturbed by the meaner side of nature. This is far from reality. From October to April, depressions regularly sweep in from the Atlantic, bringing gales as fierce as any experienced in northern waters. The strongest winds usually blow from the west but, on occasions when a depression passes to the south of the area, the wind direction is reversed. This was the state of affairs when the small convoy left Algeciras Bay on the 420-mile passage to Algiers.

Shortly after rounding Europa Point, the *Garlinge* found herself steaming into the teeth of a force 6 easterly wind, which was whipping up a rough head sea. Although her ageing engine was determinedly making revolutions for 10 knots, her progress through the water was reduced to a bare 5 knots as she dipped her blunt bows into a sea growing higher by the hour. Very soon, she began to drop astern of the convoy and was in danger of becoming a straggler. The convoy commodore, unwilling to lose almost a quarter of the cargo in his charge, from time to time reduced the speed of the convoy, in order that the *Garlinge* might keep pace with the others. But, by nightfall on the 9th, the man's patience had been tried too much and, signalling the Welsh ship to proceed independently, he ordered the convoy's speed increased to $6\frac{1}{2}$ knots. The labouring collier slowly fell astern and the darkness folded around her.

Philosophically accepting the situation as beyond his control, Captain Barnes maintained his course and speed, determined at all costs to deliver his cargo of coal to the Americans, who were by now ashore in Algiers. As the night progressed, there was no improvement in the weather, the wind remaining strong from the east and the rough sea continuing to buffet the small ship with undiminished ferocity. Although the visibility was good, the night was moonless and black enough for Barnes to be confident his ship would be able to struggle along unseen by hostile eyes until daylight. He left the bridge in charge of the officer of the watch and went below to rest while the opportunity was at hand.

Chief Officer Robert Macmillan had the middle watch, from midnight to four, on the morning of the 10th. At 00.45, he fixed the position of the *Garlinge* as twenty-one miles due north of Cape Ivi, a low headland backed by the massive peaks of the Atlas Mountains. The port of Algiers lay 180 miles to the east, another thirty-three hours steaming, assuming there was no moderation in the weather. Unhappily, the fate of the *Garlinge* was not to rest solely with the weather for, as Macmillan plotted his position on the chart, Friedrich Guggenberger was moving *U-81* into attack.

The torpedo struck the *Garlinge* in her port side between the engineroom and the stokehold; it was a classic U-boat strike, designed to cause the maximum damage below the waterline. The 800 pound charge of high explosive lifted the small ship bodily out of the water, at the same time ripping her hull wide open. Her labouring engine stopped and a great cloud of steam and smoke shot up from her stokehold to envelop the bridge. Captain Barnes, wide awake, reached the wheelhouse within seconds of the explosion.

A hurried inspection soon revealed to Barnes the enormity of the damage. The engineroom was finished, completely wrecked and flooding rapidly. The tall funnel, sheared off at its base, was leaning at an angle of 45 degrees, held only by its stays, while the port lifeboat had gone, reduced to matchwood by the blast. The ship had taken a pronounced port list, which was increasing with alarming speed. Barnes realized that the *Garlinge*, his first command, had very little time left.

While Barnes gathered up the ship's confidential books and hurled them over the side in their weighted bag, Chief Officer Macmillan mustered what crew he could find and began lowering the remaining lifeboat. It was too late. Before the boat reached the water, the *Garlinge* gave a sickening lurch and capsized. Barnes, who was still on the bridge, was dragged under with his sinking ship. Deeper and deeper he went into the black water until his lungs were on the point of bursting; then, miraculously untouched by the tangled rigging and falling wreckage, he shot to the surface. Shaking his head to clear the water from his eyes, he was relieved to see the dark outline of a liferaft tossing on the water nearby.

Battling his way through the rough sea, Barnes clambered gratefully aboard the raft, which he found was already occupied by the *Garlinge*'s senior radio officer Charles Ball. Once aboard and able to survey the wreckage-strewn sea around him, he saw clusters of red lifejacket lights bobbing on the water indicating the presence of other survivors. Working quickly, Barnes and the radio officer dragged onto the raft seven men who were close by in the water, but when they attempted to paddle towards lights seen further off, they could make no headway against the sea.

In a little while, the nine remaining men clinging precariously to the tiny wooden refuge sighted one of the convoy's escorting trawlers and it seemed their night of horror would soon be ended. But, in spite of their cries for help and a smoke float set off by Barnes, the trawler passed by apparently without seeing them.

Daylight came on the 10th and, for the men on the pitching liferaft, more hope and more cruel disappointment. On two separate occasions an aircraft flew over them but took no notice of their frenzied waving or their smoke floats. The morale of the small band of survivors sank to a new low. Five more miserable hours passed then, just before mid-day, their hopes were again raised by the sight of another trawler on the horizon. This time it was rescue. HMS *Minna* one of the escort trawlers, had come back for them.

Minna first picked up five men from two other rafts floating in the vicinity and then took on board Barnes and the others. She continued to search and, four hours later, sixteen hours after the *Garlinge* had taken her sudden plunge, Chief Officer

Macmillan was found clinging to two wooden hatchboards and was also plucked from the sea. But he was the last man to be found. Of the *Garlinge*'s crew of 40 only 15 survived. Twenty-five men, including her Second Officer, Chief, Second and Third Engineers, Second Radio Officer and seven gunners had perished. For Captain William Barnes, his first voyage in command and his involvement in Operation Torch had ended in outrageous bad fortune and ultimate tragedy.

The landing of British and American troops on the Algiers beachheads began shortly after 01.00 on 8 November. There was some delay and confusion due to the inexperienced Americans landing in the wrong positions but, fortunately, the opposition put up by the Vichy French was unco-ordinated and far from strong. Elsewhere, at Casablanca and Oran, the story was very similar. Operation Torch had been an unqualified success and was to lead six months later to the surrender of 250,415 German and Italian troops. The Axis adventure in North Africa was over. In the initial days of Operation Torch, when 90,000 men and their equipment were put ashore, only one Allied merchant ship was sunk, the unfortunate *Garlinge*.

Kapitän-Leutnant Friedrich Guggenberger reached the peak of his career with the sinking of the *Garlinge*. He was to send only five more ships to the bottom, before being taken prisoner when in command of *U-513*, which was sunk by aircraft off the coast of Brazil in July 1943. After the war, Guggenberger remained with the German Navy, retiring with the rank of rear-admiral. *U-81* also ran out of luck with the torpedoing of the Welsh ship. She returned to the Mediterranean in January 1943 under the command of Oberleutnant Johann Krieg but was able to account for only two ships and a handful of small coasters, before being destroyed by Allied aircraft while alongside her berth in Pola, Yugoslavia, a year later.

15

The Queen City: Christmas in the South Atlantic

Of all the great oceans, the South Atlantic is the most well-behaved and is regarded by seamen to be a fair weather run for much of the year. The North Atlantic is constantly swept by malicious storms summer and winter, the Indian Ocean is plagued by the miserable Southwest Monsoon from April to September and even the supposedly benign Pacific feels the savage lash of the typhoon and cyclone sporadically throughout the year. North of the Roaring Forties, the South Atlantic, being devoid of large islands which can trigger drifting masses of unstable air into malevolent cyclonic disturbances, has a weather pattern that is both predictable and pleasant. It is affected only by the Southeast Trades, so eagerly sought after by the windjammers of yesterday. The benevolent winds, resulting from a permanent high pressure system centred over the area, blow across the ocean from the Cape of Good Hope to the Equator. They are constant in direction and rarely stronger than force 5 on the Beaufort Scale, which is no more than a fresh breeze to the seaman. With them the Trades bring blue skies dotted with fair-weather cumulus and sunrises and sunsets whose beauty once seen is never forgotten. It was into these halcyon waters that Reardon Smith's *Queen City* set sail in the closing days of 1942.

Commanded by Captain G. Hornsby, the 4,814-ton *Queen City* left Capetown on 1 December with 7,900 tons of general cargo destined for the island of Trinidad. Her intended course followed the great circle track to a point midway between Cabo San Roque on the east coast of Brazil, and Atol das Rocas some 120 miles off the mainland and 4 degrees south of the Equator. From there she would parallel the Brazilian coast west-northwestwards to her destination. The total distance to steam was 5,315 miles. At the fifteen year old *Queen City*'s average speed of $9\frac{1}{4}$ knots, this would be a passage of twenty-four days, culminating – so it was hoped by all on board – in an arrival in Trinidad on Christmas Day.

For Hornsby and his crew, the passage ahead had all the makings of a peace time trans-ocean cruise, for these were waters where the drums of war were so muted as to be almost inaudible. For those on board who remembered the terrible mauling the ship suffered at the hands of the German bombers off Kinnaird Head in the autumn of 1940, the prospect of a peaceful run was doubly welcome. But there was the inevitable talk of German surface raiders being at sea and on the lookout for merchantmen sailing unescorted, as was the *Queen City*. Such talk was well-founded for, since the outset of the war the South Atlantic had been a lucrative hunting ground for the raiders. The *Graf Spee*, the *Admiral Scheer*, the *Atlantis* and many others had passed this way, leaving in their wake a substantial string of Allied merchant ships resting on the bottom.

Although he was unaware of the fact, Captain Hornsby had little cause to worry in the matter of surface raiders. Following the sinking of the *Stier*, the *Komet* and the *Thor* in quick succession in the preceeding three months, the German Naval Staff had decided to abandon any further ventures in this line. The bailiwick of the South Atlantic had now passed into the hands of Admiral Dönitz who, true to form, had wasted no time in bringing in his U-boats. Long before the *Queen City* sailed from Capetown, nine U-boats had taken up station off the Brazilian coast. With them was the Italian submarine *Tazzoli*, commanded by Carlo Fecia di Cossato, both of whom had played a large part in the spectacular rescue of the crew of the raider *Atlantis*. Dönitz's South Atlantic U-boat force was supported by a 'milch cow', a 1,700-ton U-tanker which was to refuel them off the lonely St Paul's Rocks.

The Italian submarines, which had been operating in the Atlantic in conjunction with the Kriegsmarine since August 1940, had not really achieved any great success and were, in fact, regarded by Dönitz with little more than contempt. It would seem that, as in the rest of Mussolini's fighting forces, the Italian submariners were not over enthusiastic for their task. Conditions prevailing on board the Italian boats may have had a lot to do with this. Officers and men were strictly segregated, even to the extent of separate galleys, with a wide disparity in the food served. There is no doubt the officers lived on the edge of luxury, while the ratings had to be contend with the other end of the scale. This was in strict contrast to life in British and German submarines, where all ranks shared equally the discomforts of life under water. Fecia di Cossato may have been the exception that disproves the rule. Although the class division aboard the *Tazzoli* was equally as bad as in other Italian submarines, Fecia di Cossato's men worshipped him. It is probable that, as a result of this relationship he had been able to sink 13 Allied ships, totalling 73,082 tons in the twenty months he had commanded the *Tazzoli*.

On the long, lonely leg of the passage from Capetown to the Brazilian coast, the *Queen City*'s wireless operators intercepted a number of transmissions indicating U-boats were abroad in the area, but no confirmation or diversionary signals were received from the Admiralty. Following the old adage that no news is good news, Captain Hornsby continued on his planned course. The ocean was big, his ship small and, for much of the passage, the chances of her being sighted by a patrolling U-boat were rare. When she neared the Brazilian coast, the situation would be altered. Then would be the time for the *Queen City* to look to her defences. These were much the same as carried by any British merchantmen of the day, a 4-inch anti-submarine gun aft, a 12-pounder and 4 Hotchkiss machine guns. These guns were maintained and manned by four DEMS naval gunners and two men of the Maritime Anti-aircraft Regiment. It was unlikely the ship would be able to win a gun battle with the enemy but, given the opportunity, she would sell herself dearly.

It was perhaps just as well Hornsby was not aware that, as he continued to steam confidently to the northwest, another Welsh merchant ship was bringing to an end her long career in the vicinity of St Paul's Rocks, a ridge of guano covered basalt 500 miles off the coast of Brazil. The 4,358-ton *East Wales*, owned by Gibbs & Co. (West Wales Steamship Co.) was torpedoed by *U-159* on 16 December and sank, taking with her 17 of her crew. Like the *Queen City*, the *East Wales* had also survived the bombs of a German aircraft off the British coast in 1940. Many a superstitutious man might have drawn a parallel here.

Twenty days out of Capetown, the *Queen City* had rounded the northeastern bulge of South America and was steaming west-northwest at about 250 miles off the Brazilian coast. It was four days before Christmas and she was just 890 miles from the West Indian island of Trinidad. The weather was fine, the horizon clear and a favourable moderate breeze blowing from astern. At sunset she sailed serenely into Fecia di Cossato's sights.

The first torpedo struck on the starboard side, immediately under the *Queen City*'s bridge. There was a blinding flash, a deafening explosion and a huge column of water was thrown into the air to casade down on those who stood transfixed on the open bridge. Before Hornsby could collect his shattered wits, a second torpedo tore into the fore end of No. 4 hold, the explosion blowing the wooden hatch covers and tarpaulins skywards. Both lifeboats on the starboard side of the boat deck were smashed by the blast.

Within a few seconds, the *Queen City*, her engineroom and three of her holds open to the sea, took a heavy list to starboard. Acting quickly, for he knew he had little time, Hornsby gave the order to abandon ship. Fortunately, only a moderate sea was running and the two lifeboats on the port side were lowered without difficulty. Both boats, containing the *Queen City*'s entire crew of 45, all uninjured, were clear of the sinking ship seven minutes after she had been hit.

Shortly after firing her second torpedo, the *Tazzoli* surfaced about a quarter of a mile off the *Queen City*'s starboard bow. Fecia di Cossato waited until the lifeboats had rowed well clear, then moved his craft round to the port side of the ship and opened fire with his deck gun at point blank range. The gun cracked seven times, each shell finding its mark in the battered hull of the Welsh ship. Ten minutes after receiving the first torpedo, the *Queen City* rolled upright and sank with dignity on an even keel.

With a lump in his throat as big as an apple, Hornsby turned his head away from the death of his ship to run his eyes dispassionately over the submarine as it motored towards his boat. She was a sleek, newly-painted craft, well over 200 feet long, he estimated, and of about 2,000 tons displacement. She had two deck guns, and the green, white and red flag of Italy flew at the after end of her large conning tower. Most of her crew appeared to have come on deck, no doubt to gloat over their victims. Two, with blonde hair, could have been Germans, for they stood out in stark contrast to the short, dark Italians. Fecia di Cossato was easily recognizable as the submarine's commander. Although no more than 5' 6" tall and dressed only in nondescript blue shorts and shirt, his fierce black beard and aggressive air of authority left nothing to doubt.

As the submarine drew near, Hornsby steeled himself to face the second ordeal of the night. Since early in the war, it had been the enemy's policy to, whenever possible, take prisoner the master and, sometimes, the senior officers of a torpedoed ship. There was sound reasoning behind this policy for, as far as British ships were concerned, experienced senior men were irreplaceable, except over a long period. Hornsby considered it his plain duty to avoid capture and, indeed, having got his men safely off the *Queen City* without loss or injury, it was his firm intention to see them personally to the safety of the nearest land. Providentially, when his ship had been taken so rudely from under him, he had been wearing, as he was now, khaki shirt and shorts with no epaulettes of rank. In a lifeboat crowded with 23 men he could pass as a nobody.

When Fecia di Cossato brought his submarine close to Hornsby's lifeboat, he called for the captain of the ship to identify himself. Hornsby, taking the bull by the horns and posing as a rating, replied that the captain was not in the boat and his wherabouts were not known. In answer to questions regarding the ship's officers he gave the same reply. The act was successful for, somewhat naïvely, the Italian commander seemed to accept that the lifeboat contained only ratings and backed the *Tazzoli* away. One can only assume he believed the British Merchant Navy to be run on the same strictly segregated lines, with officers in one lifeboat and ratings in another.

However, the bearded Italian met with no better success when he went alongside the other boat. This time he asked for the chief engineer and was again outwitted, for the *Queen City*'s chief, seeing the submarine approaching, had quickly peeled off his uniform jacket and sat on it, remaining inconspicious thereafter. A sailor in the boat took up the cue and informed the Italian that the chief engineer had gone down with the ship. Frustrated but determined not to leave empty handed, Fecia di Cossato then picked out one of the survivors, who happened to be a steward, and ordered him aboard the submarine. He then handed over 400 cigarettes to those in the boat and then made off.

Watching the *Tazzoli* motor away towards the horizon, Hornsby breathed a large sigh of relief and then turned his mind to the problems of survival. The *Queen City*'s wireless transmitter had been smashed by the explosion of the first torpedo and there had been no chance for her operator to send out a distress call. Fortunately, however, the ship's lifeboat radio, a cumbersome affair contained in a large waterproofed suitcase – which Fecia di Cossato, for his own safety, should have confiscated – was safe in the boat and in working order. As soon as the Italian submarine was out of sight, Hornsby instructed the wireless operator to send out a distress message, giving the position of the sinking of the *Queen City*. After seven transmissions of less than two minutes each, the battery of the transmitter was found to be flat.

Realizing it was most unlikely his call for help had been heard in such a short time, Hornsby was now faced with a life or death decision. He could keep his lifeboats drifting in the vicinity of the sinking and wait to be picked up by a passing ship, or make an attempt to reach land. He calculated the nearest land, the northern coast of Brazil in the region of St Luiz, lay some 210 miles to the south. This was a formidible distance for the open, barge-like lifeboats to sail under the equatorial sun. Had they been in more frequented waters, he would have been content to stream sea anchors and wait for rescue, but this was an empty part of the ocean. Better to die in the attempt to reach land, Hornsby decided, than to end up as dehydrated corpses drifting in the slough of their own hopelessness. At 18.30, one hour after disaster had struck the *Queen City*, Hornsby put his chief officer in charge of the second boat and they hoisted sail and headed south for Brazil. Chief Officer Tarr's boat proved to be the better sailer for, within two hours, it had pulled so far ahead that Hornsby had lost sight of it in the darkness. He was not to see it again.

An examination of the lockers and tanks in Hornsby's boat revealed it was well provisioned. There was a good supply of condensed milk, Horlicks tablets and pemmican, while the fresh water tanks were full. However, uncertain of how long they would take to reach the land, Hornsby prudently rationed the water to 2 full dippers, or about one third of a pint, per man per day. There was a fair sailing wind and, although the ungainly boat's speed was no more than 4 knots, progress was steady and in the right direction. The nights were cool but the days, with the sun almost directly overhead, were unbearably hot. Most of the survivors were clad only in shorts and shirt and, as there was very little shade in the boat, they suffered the agonies of sunburn. In spite of this, there was little sign of despondency.

At about 21.00 on the night of 23 December, after sailing steadily for just over fifty hours, the lights of the shore were sighted. Hornsby approached the land warily and, after judging the breakers to be too big for a safe landing at night, decided to stand off until daylight. Setting sail again at dawn, the boat eventually grounding on a shelving beach at four o'clock in the afternoon. It was Christmas Eve.

Discovering they had landed at Guimaraes, a small fishing village thirty-five miles to the west of the port of St Luiz, Hornsby's first action after stepping ashore was to find a telephone and contact the British Consul in that port. Transportation by land in this remote corner of Brazil being impracticable, the Consul agreed to send a tug. That afternoon, for the second time in seventy-two hours, Hornsby and his men boarded their lifeboat and were towed to St Luiz, where they arrived next morning, the 25th. This was a Christmas Day none of them would ever forget.

The *Queen City*'s other lifeboat, in charge of Chief Officer A. H. Tarr, had not fared so well. Although it had appeared to be the faster of the two boats, it had in fact made considerable leeway on its 240 mile passage. Tarr and his men spent their Christmas at sea, finally coming ashore on an even more remote beach fifty-eight miles to the east of St Luiz. They were fortunate enough to find a spring of water after landing and lived a fairly comfortable Robinson Crusoe-like existence for two days, before they were able to contact St Luiz through some local fishermen. The same tug that had rescued their shipmates towed them into St Luiz on the 28th.

The *Tazzoli*'s subsequent career was short and unfruitful. She was to sink only one more ship before she was herself destroyed by a British aircraft in the Bay of Biscay on 16 May 1943.

16

The Llanashe: the long voyage to nowhere

January 1943 had been a bonus month for British shipping, with only 18 ships lost through enemy action, totalling a mere 91,056 tons. This was an immense improvement on the previous year, which had seen a consistent monthly loss of around 50 ships of 250,000 tons. The ships of the Red Dragon had fared even better. In January not a single Welsh ship had fallen to the enemy's axe. Tentatively, the question as being asked if this was the turning of the tide; the long awaited emergence from darkness into light.

The month was drawing to a close as Evan Thomas, Radcliffe & Co.'s *Llanashe* left the Iraqi port of Basrah and began her long, tortuous passage down the Shatt al Arab waterway to the sea. Ahead of her lay a lonely voyage of 6,000 miles, during which she would be the potential prey of German and Japanese submarines and surface raiders. With a maximum speed of $9\frac{1}{2}$ knots and an armament consisting only of a 4.7-inch stern gun and 4 light machine guns, she was an odds-on favourite for extinction.

The *Llanashe* was one of the newer ships in the fleet of Evan Thomas, Radcliffe & Co., the Cardiff shipowners. Built in 1936 by Bartram & Son of Sunderland, she was of 4,836 tons gross and while no ocean greyhound, she had pleasing lines for a tramp ship of her day. In her short life before the war she had carried coal from the mines of South Wales to all corners of the globe, returning, often after many months, laden with wheat, ore, sugar or whatever the charter market had to offer. In short, the *Llanashe* was a typical Welsh tramp, a no-frills moneymaker, owned and manned by men who knew the hard

s/s *Llanashe* 4836 GRT. Sunk by *U-182* off South Africa 17 February 1943.

business of the sea. Her commander, Captain James Parry of Tywyn, was one such man.

For Captain Parry, pacing the bridge of his ship as she slid past the muddy banks of the Shat al Arab – which was to be the focus of another bloody war forty years later – the long voyage ahead must have been a daunting prospect. For more than four gut-twisting years he had walked the slippery tightrope of war at sea. How much longer would his luck hold out?

The *Llanashe*'s current cargo did nothing to increase Parry's confidence in his future. She carried 3,500 tons of tinplate which, stowing at 15 cubic feet to the ton, was a deadweight cargo in every sense of the word. Should the *Llanashe*'s hull be breached, she would go to the bottom in a matter of minutes – and Parry was acutely aware that the chance of such a disaster happening must be high. Before sailing from Basrah, he had learned that the German armed merchant cruiser *Michel* was at large in the Indian Ocean and had sunk 5 Allied ships in the closing months of 1942. There was also the invisible threat of the U-boats. At any one time there were known to be at least seven German and eight Japanese submarines operating in this area. These appeared to hunt mainly in the approaches to the Persian Gulf and at the southern end of the Mozambique Channel, and Parry was prepared to meet the danger they posed to his ship. Fortunately for his peace of mind, he was not aware that five of Germany's new 'U-cruisers', each with a range of 30,000 miles, had recently broken into the Indian Ocean and were creating havoc amongst shipping rounding the Cape of Good Hope. One of their number was *U-182*, commanded by Korvetten-Kapitän Nicolai Clausen. Parry and Clausen were soon to meet, but not face to face in this world.

For two days the *Llanashe* steamed south through the Persian Gulf with the temperature steadily climbing – much to the delight of all on board. Basrah in January had been a cold, cheerless place. Off Bandar Abbas, Iran's port at the southern end of the Gulf, the *Llanashe* joined up with a convoy which was to take her through the Straits of Hormuz and clear of the dangerous sector of the Arabian Sea where the U-boats were in the habit of setting up ambush. Three days out of Bandar Abbas, when abeam of the Omani island of Masira, she left the convoy and set out alone on her long haul to the Cape.

The direct route from the Straits of Hormuz to South Africa passes close to the lonely island of Socotra and south through the Mozambique Channel, which separates Madagascar from the African mainland. It is a distance of some 4,500 miles. In more normal times, the *Llanashe* would have taken this route, rubbing shoulders with the elite cargo liners trading regularly between South Africa and the Indian sub-continent. These were, of course, not normal times and in the early summer of 1942, Japanese submarines had congregated in the southern approaches to the Mozambique Channel and, in two short months, sank 24 Allied merchantmen, totalling 127,261 tons. This had been an unforseen massacre which rocked the Admiralty back on their heels and sent them scurrying to their charts seeking a safer route to and from the Cape. In consequence, Captain Parry now laid his courses in a wide parabola, curving first to the southeast to pass between the Chagos Archipelago and the Seychelles, then south to Rodriquez Island, southwest to a point 300 miles clear of the southern tip of Madagascar, and so to the Cape of Good Hope. This wide diversion added more than 800 miles to the passage – an extra $3\frac{1}{2}$ to 4 days steaming for the *Llanashe* – but it was a precaution Parry could not afford to ignore.

Crossing the Equator in early February, the *Llanashe* moved into the largely deserted waters of the South Indian Ocean. For the time being, the immediate danger of attack by U-boat was past, but Parry dare not relax his vigilance. Zig-zagging by day and holding a straight course at night, he pushed his ship southwards at her maximum $9\frac{1}{2}$ knots. By the 16th she was clear of the danger area off the Mozambique Channel and heading southwest for the Cape. Late that evening, Parry received a wireless message from the Admiralty directing him to proceed to Port Elizabeth and there join a convoy for Cape-town. The distance between these two ports being a mere 420 miles, it must have been obvious to Parry that U-boats were now active off the Cape.

At 22.00 that night, the *Llanashe* came around onto a more westerly course, heading for Port Elizabeth and the shelter of the convoy escorts – such as they were in this remote sphere of the war. The Cape summer had now taken an unusual turn and it was blowing a near-gale from the north, with a rough, confused sea. The night was black, the sky clear and the visibility good. Conditions could not have been better for Nicolai Clausen, who was lying in wait with his torpedo tubes loaded. The *Llanashe* was only 170 miles to the east of Port Elizabeth when, at 02.45 on the morning of the 17th, she was struck by a torpedo on her starboard just abaft the engineroom. Chief Officer Samuel Lloyd, who was enjoying his last hour of fitful sleep before taking up his watch at 04.00, was awoken by a dull thud. Automatically, he tumbled out of his bunk and reached for his lifejacket. When Lloyd reached the deck, he realized at once that his ship had been struck a fatal blow. No 4 cargo hold, immediately abaft the engineroom, was wide open to the night, its tarpaulins, hatchboards and steel beams having been blown skywards by the force of the explosion. One tarpaulin, 800 square feet of heavy canvas, had been caught on the truck of the mainmast and was noisily thrashing itself to shreds in the wind like some gigantic storm ensign.

The steady beat of the *Llanashe*'s engine had ceased and she appeared to be settling rapidly by the stern. All the signs were that the torpedo had hit near to the watertight bulkhead separating the engine spaces from No. 4 hold and both these huge compartments were now open to the sea. As Lloyd struggled to take in the full horror of the situation, the order came from the bridge to abandon ship. He ran to the boat deck to supervise the lowering of the lifeboat in his charge. The *Llanashe* carried four lifeboats, two on each side of the vessel with ample capacity for her 42-man crew. All boats were fitted with solid skates, or wrap-around fenders to protect them from damage against the ship's side when being lowered in a seaway. On this wild night, the sea was running high and, although Lloyd was able to get his boat down to the water without damage, as soon as it hit the waves it began to slam heavily against the ship's side. In spite of the skates, wood splintered on steel and Lloyd realized that unless the rope painter holding the boat alongside was cast off quickly, the boat would be pounded to pieces in a matter of minutes.

Showing considerable courage and presence of mind, Lloyd grasped one of the lifelines rigged between the davits and launched himself outwards, sliding down the rope as he went. It was his intention to cut the boat free before it was damaged beyond use. As he neared the water, the boat reared up on a wave and sheered away from the ship's side. He made a desperate jump but landed short of the boat and plunged into the raging sea.

In February, which is the southern summer, the sea off the coast of South Africa is warm, averaging around 70 degrees Fahrenheit. To Lloyd, on this night when the world had fallen about his ears, the seething water must surely have resembled a clammy shroud as it enveloped him and dragged him deep. The fear that he was being pulled down with his sinking ship sent panic running through his veins and he kicked out, fighting his way back to the surface. When his head finally broke water, he found himself alone in a hostile ocean. The lifeboat had disappeared, smashed and sunk, or swept away by the angry sea. There were no comforting voices borne on the wind, no bobbing lights, nothing but a dull, red glow silhouetting the dying *Llanashe* as, weighed down by 3,500 tons of tinplate in her bottom, she slid beneath the waves stern first.

After about forty-five minutes in the water, Lloyd saw a dark shape nearby rising and falling on the waves. Gratefully, he swam towards it. It was a liferaft, a small, wooden thing, 6 feet by 6 feet and floating perilously low in the water. Heaving himself aboard, Lloyd found the raft already occupied. The *Llanashe*'s Second Officer, Robert Bressey, her chief steward, Suetaka Saito and a DEMS gunlayer named Hodder lay huddled in a wretched heap on the boards of the tiny craft. They were all alive but wet, miserable and exhausted. Lloyd's arrival on the already overcrowded raft did nothing to improve their situation.

What had been a near-gale viewed from the comparative safety of the *Llanashe*'s boat deck, was a full-blown storm here at sea level. The wind screamed and angry, green-crested waves broke over the raft, constantly threatening to tear the four men from their precarious perch. The thought crossed Lloyd's mind that he might have been better off going down with his ship. As far as he could remember from the chart, they were at least eighty miles from the nearest land. Other ships did come this way but they were infrequent and the possibility of the half-submerged raft being sighted in this turbulent sea was very slim. And all the while, the fury of the northerly wind was pushing them slowly but relentlessly south into the grey, empty wastes of the great Southern Ocean, where nothing but the giant albatross and the iceberg moved. There had been no opportunity to send a distress message before the ship went down, so there could be no hope of assistance from the shore, where their plight was, as yet, unknown. Only when the *Llanashe* had been several days overdue would a search be organized. Under the conditions prevailing that might be too late.

Lloyd had been some ten minutes on the liferaft when *U-182* surfaced to verify her kill. Lloyd watched fascinated as the submarine neared the raft, his ship-orientated mind subconsciously taking note of her appearance. She was very large, with two guns on deck, one forward and one aft. Her square-shaped conning tower was crowded with men wearing heavy, duffle-type coats. Obviously, as many of *U-182*'s crew as possible had come on deck to witness the results of their night's work. The raft bumped alongside the submarine's casing, bringing Lloyd to his first, and only, meeting with the man responsible for his predicament, Korvetten-Kapitän Nicolai Clausen. Leaning over the fore end of the conning tower, Clausen cupped his hands and called to the men on the raft, demanding the name and destination of his victim. Lloyd who, with his ship on the bottom could see no virtue in being a silent hero, answered truthfully. Unfortunately, Clausen's English was limited and he was completely baffled by Lloyd's strong, West Walian accent. For several minutes, the two men, bawling above the noise of the wind and waves, held a nonsensical shouting match which would have been hilarious in any other circumstances. Eventually, Clausen seemed to grasp the name of the ship but was not prepared to bandy more words. He backed his submarine away and made off at full speed, leaving the men on the raft to their fate.

It may be that Clausen's frustration swamped his more humane feelings for, in retrospect, it is hard to understand why he offered no help for the four men on the raft, who were in an obviously desperate situation. Given that he was unable to take the men on board the U-boat, a small supply of food and water passed down to them would have been a gesture of mercy which, as it transpired, might have made all the difference between life and death for many in the days to follow.

For Lloyd and the others, the remainder of the night was a half-remembered nightmare of abject misery. The day dawned at last, and with it came a ray of hope. Three other liferafts were in sight on the heaving sea, all carrying survivors. With great difficulty the four rafts were manoeuvred alongside each other and lashed together. Including Lloyd and his companions, there were now sixteen men, among them Chief Engineer David Harries, Second Radio Officer R. Thompson and an Army gunner named Woodrow. They were, it appeared, all that remained of the *Llanashe*'s crew of forty-two.

Lloyd, being the senior officer, took charge, determined to make the best of a bad situation. He distributed the men as comfortably as possible on the rafts and then took stock of the provisions available. Each raft was equipped with watertight tanks, which should have contained standard lifeboat rations and fresh water. To the survivors' horror, they found the tanks of three of the liferafts completely empty, while those of the fourth raft yielded only one tin of Horlicks tablets, two tins of chocolate and half a gallon of water. The thieves of the Basrah dockside had been at work.

The flame of hope kindled by the coming together of the liferafts spluttered and all but died. But there was worse to come. In the next twenty-four hours, the weather deteriorated further and the heavily laden rafts were frequently capsized, throwing their occupants into the water. Although the sea was still comparatively warm, the continual struggle to stay aboard the rafts began to take its toll. The Horlicks tablets, which should have given the men the energy to fight, served only to increase their thirst and the tin was therefore reluctantly consigned to the deep. Lloyd then set the rations at one piece of chocolate and half a dipper of water per day per man. For men already suffering from shock and exposure, this was only a token offering to the gods of survival.

The tiny, waterlogged flotilla drifted aimlessly, battered by the wind and waves. There was no shelter from the burning sun during the day and only cold and dampness at night. The rafts heaved and tossed without let-up and, with the exception of Lloyd and the gunlayer Hodder, one by one the men succumbed to an awful wretching seasickness that would not go away. This sickness, which only those who have suffered it can appreciate, combined with the extremes of temperature and lack of sustenance, so weakened the survivors that they became light-headed and without hope. Ironically, the sea around them teemed with fish but, without hooks and lines to catch them, these might just as well have been part of some cruel mirage. The odd flying fish that flopped aboard was immediately torn apart and eaten raw but there were too few to tip the scales.

For one brief, ecstatic moment hopes of rescue ran high, when an aircraft was seen flying low over the water. But the plane flew off without approaching the rafts and the survivors fell into a new trough of despondency.

Lloyd and Hodder, who seemed to be able to draw on each other's strength, worked hard to stem the tide of despair threatening to engulf the rafts. They worked in vain. The others were too far gone to be chivvied into fighting for their lives. On the fifth day after the sinking of the *Llanashe*, Second Officer Robert Bressey went quietly mad and died.

By the ninth day, the rafts had broken adrift and there was neither the will nor the strength to bring them together again. Lloyd, Hodder and Chief Steward Suetaka Saito were once more alone on the wide unyielding ocean. All three were desperately weak and Saito, the quiet Cardiff-domiciled Japanese, rambling and obviously near to death. Lloyd and Hodder, determined to live at all costs, resorted to an elaborate fantasy, plying each other with imaginary plates of steaming food and glasses of ice-cold beer. For them, the illusion worked but Saito was beyond such childish guile. On the morning of the tenth day he was found to be dead and was slipped over the side. Twenty-four hours later, the last of the meagre rations were eaten and the two remaining survivors, finally accepting the inevitable, crouched on the heaving raft awaiting the oblivion of death.

Late on 27 February, the British motor vessel *Tarrakan*, manned by a Dutch crew, was approaching Port Elizabeth from the east, intent on joining a Capetown-bound convoy. For some reason, possibly because it was a black, unfriendly night, the master of the *Tarrakan* decided against entering Algoa Bay in darkness. After sighting the lights of the port, he steamed back out to sea to await daylight.

As the first rays of the sun were paling the eastern horizon, a keen-eyed lookout on the *Tarrakan* sighted three liferafts rising and falling on the long rollers. From two of the liferafts the Dutchmen picked up only bodies but on the third there was life. Chief Officer Samuel Lloyd and Gunlayer Hodder, unconscious and their emaciated bodies covered with salt water sores, were gently lifted into a cargo net and hoisted aboard the *Tarrakan*. They were landed at Capetown on 4 March, where they spent seven weeks in hospital recovering from their terrible ordeal.

Eleven other survivors of the sinking of the *Llanashe* were rescued from a lifeboat off the fishing village of Knysna, having been carried a distance of 260 miles by the Aghulas Current, which sweeps westwards around the Cape. Of the ship's total crew of forty-two, twenty-nine had perished, including Captain James Parry, whose luck had finally run out.

Nicolai Clausen outlived James Parry by three months. Following the despatch of the *Llanashe*, he embarked on a long and unrewarding patrol off the Mozambique channel, sinking only one ship in two months. He then returned to the North Atlantic where on 16 May 1943, *U-182* was caught while harrassing a convoy and destroyed by the American escort vessel *Mackenzie*. Clausen and his men perished.

17

The Clarissa Radcliffe: the last great battle

In mid-January 1943, Churchill and Roosevelt had one of their rare face-to-face meetings. The venue was Casablanca, the subject the invasion of the enemy's territory by joint Anglo-American forces. In Russia, the German Sixth Army was frozen into immobility before Stalingrad and threatened with extinction, while in North Africa, Rommel was caught in the jaws of a pincer movement set up by Montgomery and Eisenhower. The time was ripe for the opening of the 'Second Front' Stalin had been urging for so long. At Casablanca it was agreed to tackle Sicily and Italy first and then the massive assault across the English Channel, probably in the late spring of 1944. However, before any move was made into Europe, it was first necessary to transport across the broad hazardous reaches of the North Atlantic a vast American army, together with its guns, tanks, planes and stores.

The task was a daunting one, for the battle for the Atlantic sea lanes was rapidly moving towards a new climax. Dönitz had thrown more than 100 U-boats into the fray, most of them to hunt in packs in the 'air-gap' in mid-Atlantic, where no cover could be provided for the convoys by the long-range Liberators and Sunderlands based on opposite sides of the ocean. If January had been an encouraging month for Allied shipping, then February was traumatic. A total of 63 merchant ships of 360,000 tons were sunk in this month. March was to be even worse, but if the invasion of Europe was to be a reality, there was no alternative but to increase the numbers of ships crossing the Atlantic from west to east.

Convoy under attack

In the last week of February and the first week in March, four consecutive eastbound convoys were to set out from New York. They involved a total of 193 Allied merchant ships and 38 escort vessels. Each convoy was heavily attacked in mid-Atlantic, it being estimated that as many as 70 U-boats operated against them. In all, 38 merchantmen and one destroyer escort were sunk, for the loss of only one U-boat. It was an undisputed victory for Dönitz.

The fiercest sea action of all, greater in magnitude than Trafalgar, and the last great engagement of the Battle of the Atlantic, took place from 16 to 19 March, when two eastbound convoys merged in latitude 52 degrees North, midway between Newfoundland and Ireland. In those three days, 90 merchant ships, protected by 20 escorts, fought a pitched battle with 40 plus U-boats. The weather during the battle was at its North Atlantic worst, a malignant blend of mountainous seas, fog and snowstorms, with the additional threat of drifting icebergs.

Convoy SC 122 sailed from New York on 5 March and consisted of an armada of 50 merchant ships steaming in 13 columns abreast. American naval units escorted it as far as the Grand Banks of Newfoundland where, on the 12th, the ocean escort took over for the passage across the open Atlantic. This group was a combined Anglo-American force commanded by Commander R. C. Boyle, DSO, and consisted of the destroyers HMS *Havelock* and USS *Upshur*, the frigate HMS *Swale*, the Flower Class corvettes *Buttercup*, *Godetia*, *Lavender*, *Pimpernel* and *Saxifrage*, and the American armed trawler *Campobello*. SC 122, as indicated by its prefix, was a slow convoy, destined – God and the enemy willing – to make its way across the Atlantic at $7\frac{1}{2}$ to 8 knots.

Three days after the departure of SC 122, a second convoy of 40 ships, designated HX 229, slipped past the Ambrose light tower and formed up in 11 columns in sight of the low foreshore of Long Island. HX 229 was scheduled to make the ocean passage at 10 knots and to overtake SC 122 when both convoys were within 200 miles of the west coast of Ireland,

and under the full protection of the Royal Navy and the RAF. HX 229 was joined on the 14th by its ocean escort, the destroyers *Volunteer*, *Beverley*, *Witherington* and *Mansfield* and the Flower Class corvettes *Anemone* and *Pennywort*.

In the ranks of SC 122 sailing from New York on the 5th was the Evan Thomas, Radcliffe & Co. ship *Clarissa Radcliffe*, commanded by Captain Stuart Gordon Finnes. One of the few ships of the fleet of Evan Thomas, Radcliffe & Co. to survive the First World War, the *Clarissa Radcliffe* was a steamer of 5,754 tons gross built in 1915 by Craig, Taylor & Co. of Stockton-on-Tees and named after Henry Radcliffe's only daughter. In its early days, now long past, the *Clarissa Radcliffe*'s 470 horse power engine had developed a speed of 10 knots but, twenty-eight years on, would be hard pressed to maintain the minimum of $7\frac{1}{2}$ knots proposed for the convoy. On this voyage, the veteran Welsh ship was loaded to her winter marks with a full cargo of iron ore, which would further handicap her from the moment she left the shelter of New York harbour. For Captain Finnes and his 52-man crew facing the twofold danger of a North Atlantic winter and the determination of the U-boats, the immediate future was full of forboding.

Less than thirty-six hours out of New York, shortly after clearing the shelter of the Cape Cod peninsular, SC 122 ran into the full fury of a force 10 storm, which quickly turned the orderly columns into a chaos of 50 underpowered, overloaded merchantmen desperately fighting to remain afloat and on course. Within a few hours the convoy had scattered over a wide area, with each ship hidden from the driving rain and waging its own lonely battle against the enraged elements.

The *Clarissa Radcliffe*, rolling violently through the great weight of ore low down in her holds, shipping green seas overall and barely able to maintain steerage way, soon fell astern and lost all contact with the rest of the convoy. Two days after the storm had passed, on 9 March, she was sighted by the Canadian corvette *The Pas*, which was returning to Halifax. *The Pas* advised Captain Finnes that he was only fifteen miles astern of the convoy and urged him to make every effort to rejoin. With her tall funnel pouring black smoke and her elderly engine labouring valiantly, the *Clarissa Radcliffe* pressed ahead at her best speed. Only those on the bridge knew how slim were her chances of regaining contact with SC 122.

While SC 122 had been wrestling with the storm, the Atlantic to the eastwards was becoming a vast, shifting battleground. Fifteen hundred miles to the northeast, and in even worse weather, Convoy SC 121, which had left New York ten days earlier, was under heavy attack. German intelligence had detected the sailing and proposed route of this convoy some four days earlier, with the result that Dönitz had set up an ambush of 26 U-boats in the path of the ships. The attack began on the 6th and became a five-day nightmare, played out in storm force winds accompanied by snow, rain, hail and the inevitable mountainous seas. SC 121 was initially escorted by only a small force, consisting of two American destroyers and three corvettes, one British and two Canadian. Air cover and more surface escorts were thrown in on the 9th, when the running battle had moved to within 400 miles of the west coast of Ireland. But it was too late. SC 121 had already lost 13 ships of 60,000 tons to the U-boats. Among the casualties were the Welsh ships *Nailsea Court* and *Fort Lamy*, both of which went down with heavy loss of life.

No sooner had the battle for SC 121 been broken off than, 500 miles to the southwest and directly in the path of the oncoming SC 122, the fast convoy HX 228 also came under attack. Sighted on the morning of the 10th, the 44-ship convoy suffered its first casualty that night. Over the following forty-eight hours a force of twelve to fourteen U-boats kept a running attack, but with limited success. Four merchant ships were sunk and the destroyer HMS *Harvester* lost. On the credit side for HX 228, the U-boat which had torpedoed *Harvester* was rammed and sunk by the French corvette *Aconit*.

Late on the 14th, the C-in-C U-boats in Lorient became aware of the huge armada of 110 ships crawling eastwards across the North Atlantic in two separate groups. SC 122 was by now 600 miles to the east of Newfoundland, with HX 229 only 300 miles astern and slowly closing the gap. German intelligence had intercepted and decoded messages from the commodores of both convoys, giving exact details of ships, escorts, course, speed and intentions. Dönitz at once called in more than forty U-boats, many of them fresh from the battles of SC 121 and HX 228, and formed them up in the path of the two approaching convoys.

The attack on HX 229 opened on the night of the 16th/17th, with the sinking of two merchant ships in the first hour. By the early hours of the 17th, HX 229, forging ahead at full speed, had caught up with and merged with SC 122. The two convoys now formed a great flock of slow-moving shipping, wallowing in heavy seas, thinly protected by escorts and surrounded by marauding U-boats. In all, 150 vessels, above and below the sea were to be involved in the ensuing conflict.

The visibility was good and further enhanced by bright moonlight and the Northern Lights. The U-boats were therefore able to move in on the surface with impunity. Under such ideal conditions and with an abundance of slow-moving targets, absolute slaughter was prevented only by the magnificent work of the convoy escorts, which were outnumbered two to one by the U-boats. In the hours until dawn, only 5 merchant ships were sunk and 5 others damaged.

With the coming of daylight on the 17th, the U-boat commanders seemed so confident of their impending victory that they continued to attack on the surface. They were in the 'air-gap' and, so they thought, safe from attack by long range bombers. But at noon on that day, to their great surprise, a lone Liberator of Coastal Command, flying at the extreme limit of its range, appeared over the convoy and began scattering depth charges. The U-boats, fearing the aircraft might be the first of many to come, were forced to submerge. The Liberator, some 900 miles out from its base in Northern Ireland, was able to spend only a few minutes over the convoy, but there is little doubt that this gallant effort was a severe setback to the U-boats, who had been intent on a day's uninterrupted hunting. As it was, 9 more Allied merchant ships were to go to the bottom on that day.

Dönitz finally withdrew his wolf-packs on the night of the 19th, when the convoys had moved to within 450 miles of the Irish coast and Coastal Command was able to provide almost continuous air cover. At the final reckoning, SC 122 had lost 8 of its merchant ships and the armed trawler *Campobello*, which had foundered in heavy seas. HX 229 had suffered worse, losing 13 merchant ships. On the other side, one U-boat had been sunk by Coastal Command and the escort vessels claimed 7 others damaged. It was hardly a victory for the Allies but the blood-bath had been at least contained.

One ship was still missing from Convoy SC 122. This was the *Clarissa Radcliffe*, last seen straggling fifteen miles astern of the convoy on 9 March. Lieutenant-Commander Old of HMCS *The Pas* had given the *Clarissa Radcliffe* the position of the convoy and had observed her making the attempt to catch up. What happened to the Welsh ship after that must remain for all time a matter of conjecture, although two possible explanations have been put forward.

On the afternoon of 9 March, Oberleutnant Max Kruschka in *U-621* claimed to have sighted a ship of about 6,000 tons stopped and drifting in position 53° 15′ N, 41° 05′ W. Kruschka fired 8 torpedoes at the ship, scoring two hits. The unknown vessel did not sink. Continuing his patrol, Kruschka sighted the same ship, still afloat, on several occasions but, as she was low in the water, was reluctant to use up any more of his precious stock of torpedoes. He finally watched the ship sink on the morning of the 12th. Researchers have since claimed she was the *Clarissa Radcliffe*, but the evidence does not stand up to serious examination. The position of the attack given by Kruschka is more than 1,000 miles to the northeast of the position given for the Welsh ship by *The Pas* on the morning of the 9th. That Kruschka did sight and torpedo a ship on the 9th and then watched that same ship sink on the 12th is beyond doubt. But that unfortunate ship has never been identified. She was certainly not the *Clarissa Radcliffe*.

Another unidentified cargo ship was sighted by *U-633*, commanded by Kapitan-Leutnant Heinrich Schmid. The ship, again of about 6,000 tons, was on an easterly course in position 52° 20′ N, 27° 10′ W. Schmid missed with his first salvo of three torpedoes but scored a hit with a fourth fired singly. The merchant ship sank, apparently with all hands. No ship was reported lost in this area but it seems highly unlikely that Schmid fired at a ghost.

The credit for the sinking of the *Clarissa Radcliffe* was finally given to *U-633* on the 18th, but in a revised position of 42° 00′ N, 62° 00′ W. This gives rise to more doubts, for that position is 1,500 miles to the southwest of the one given by Schmid himself when reporting his success and is, in fact, very near to the position of the *Clarissa Radcliffe* when last seen by the corvette *The Pas*. Unless the Welsh ship had been hove-to for nine days, which seems most unlikely, or Heinrich Schmid's navigation was 1,500 miles in error, again unlikely, the officially recorded graveyard of the *Clarissa Radcliffe* can hardly be correct.

It seems more likely that Captain Finnes, realizing the impossibility of catching up with Convoy SC 122, decided to proceed independently, following the shortest route to his destination. If this is indeed true, then the *Clarissa Radcliffe*, torpedoed by *U-633* on the afternoon of the 18th, probably sank only 70 miles or so to the south of where the fierce convoy battle was raging. She was also a casualty, albeit a lonely one, of the last great action in the Battle of the Atlantic. Whether Finnes and his 54 men went down with their ship, or died later in the lifeboats will never be known. The only apparent witnesses to the sinking, Heinrich Schmid and the crew of *U-633*, were themselves lost in the Bay of Biscay some seven weeks later when *U-633* was bombed and sunk by a British aircraft.

18

The Fort Mumford: the lone survivor

On 7 May 1943, a small Indian dhow, her varnished hull peeling through long exposure to sun and salt water, rounded Cape Paman and glided into Mikindani Bay, a hook-shaped indent in the coast of Tanganyika. When the dhow brought up to her anchor, she was forty-seven days out from India's Malabar Coast, having sailed almost 3,000 miles using the dying winds of the Northeast Monsoon. Among the ten men on her deck was one who, although tanned a deep brown by the tropical sun, stood out against the others. He was unmistakably European.

Seven weeks earlier on 18 March, the day on which, in another ocean, had seen the end of the *Clarissa Radcliffe*, the 7,132-ton *Fort Mumford* had sailed from Colombo bound for Aden, 2,100 miles to the west. She was carrying a cargo of military stores, including boxed aircraft and landing craft on deck, which had already crossed two oceans.

Owned by the Ministry of War Transport and managed by Sir William Reardon Smith of Cardiff, the *Fort Mumford* was a wartime replacement ship built in Canada. She carried a crew of 53, which included 5 gunners of the Maritime Anti-Aircraft Regiment and one merchant Navy gunner. Like all her sister ships in the 'Fort' class, she was a strictly functional, mass-produced ship with an all-welded hull, a standard triple-expansion steam engine of 505 horse power – which made her underpowered for her size – and cramped accommodation lacking any of the niceties found in a company built ship. But for Captain John Henry Reardon Smith she was a considerable improvement on his previous command, which had been built in the year the Titanic made her first and last voyage.

John Henry Reardon Smith, who was a nephew of the founder of the Company, had taken his share of knocks in the war and had suffered great personal tragedy. In December 1940 he had lost his youngest son Philip, an apprentice in the *Victoria City* sunk in the massacre of Convoy HX 90 off Bloody Foreland. Less than eighteen months later, Reardon Smith himself had narrowly escaped death when his command, the *Botavon*, had been torpedoed and sunk by a German aircraft off Murmansk with the loss of 21 lives.

The *Fort Mumford*'s voyage, her first, had begun in Montreal on 5 January when she was accepted from the builders by Captain Reardon Smith and his men. A 7,000-mile ballast passage to Vancouver via the Panama Canal had followed, during which the *Fort Mumford* was moulded into a Reardon Smith ship. Her working life commenced in Vancouver, where she loaded a part cargo in the depths of the British Columbian winter. Not a man aboard her was sorry when they finally closed up the hatches and set off on the long leg across the Pacific to Lyttleton in the south island of New Zealand.

In New Zealand they found an island paradise a million light years removed from the war. The South Pacific summer, the magnificent scenery and, above all, the overwhelming hospitality of the people of the island had for Reardon Smith and his men made the visit as memorable as any experienced by the seamen of Captain Cook's day. For some, the temptation proved to much. Worn down perhaps by the stress of seagoing in wartime and dazzled by the contrast this beautiful island presented to a drab, austere Britain, four of the *Fort Mumford*'s crew deserted in Lyttleton. And who could blame them?

The month-long passage around the under-belly of Australia and across an Indian Ocean lying blue and quiescent under the North-East Monsoon was, for Reardon Smith and many of the older men aboard, reminiscent of those days of peace when their only adversary had been the sea itself. A few hours in Colombo taking bunkers and then, on the morning of 18 March, the *Fort Mumford* turned her bows westward. When he took his ship of out the breakwaters of Colombo Harbour, Reardon Smith looked forward with confidence to at least another week of trouble free steaming. He had been advised that any U-boats at large in the Arabian Sea would most likely to be concentrated off Cape Guardifui, near to the eastern approaches to the Gulf of Aden. There was time enough to worry about them.

With her dark outline betrayed only by the phosphorescence of her bow wave, the *Fort Mumford* slipped past Cape Cormorin, the southernmost point of India, on the night of the 19th and came round onto a west-northwesterly course. She was bound through the Nine Degree Channel, the wide gap between the Laccadive and Maldive Islands, which straddle the way to the East like a broken string of pearls. On the other side of the islands lay the Arabian Sea, once a bloody battleground of pirates and East Indiamen, now host only to the leisurely dhow and the occasional hurrying, grey-painted merchantmen.

Sunset on the 20th saw the *Fort Mumford* 90 miles due west of Suheli Par, southernmost islet of the Laccadives. She was steaming at 9 knots through a flat calm sea, with no breath of wind, other than that she was making, to flush out the heat of the day from her accommodation. With the coming of dusk, hazy conditions closed in, restricting visibility, but the officer of the watch on the bridge was not disturbed. Very little traffic was expected in this area.

An hour later, below decks, Seaman Gunner Horace Bailey lay on the top of his bunk in the cabin he shared with two Army gunners. The room was stiflingly hot and Bailey heaved a sigh of relief when the other men gathered up their gear and made for the door. It was 20.00; time to change the watch.

For Toshiaki Fukumura, commander of the Japanese submarine *I-27*, the patrol so far had been an adject failure. Days of combing the Arabian Sea, on the surface at night and submerged during daylight, had revealed nothing more than the occasional native dhow scurrying along under full sail. Disappointment and frustration were consuming him but he feared most the loss of face he would suffer if he returned to Japan with his torpedoes unused. Then, shortly before 20.00 on 20 March, Fukumura's luck changed. Out of the hazy darkness loomed a large merchant ship, loaded to her marks and her decks piled up high with cargo.

The torpedo struck the *Fort Mumford* as the last tones of eight bells rang out from her bridge. Simultaneous with the deafening explosion, Horace Bailey glimpsed a vivid flash through the porthole near to his head. Before he had time to collect his scattered wits, the ship gave a violent lurch to port, throwing him out of his bunk. Still dazed, he got to his feet and scrambled for the door of the cabin. No alarm bells had been sounded but he knew the ship must have been torpedoed, probably in the engineroom.

Bailey fought his way out of the gunners' accommodation through an escape hatch, which was partially blocked by a jumble of planks and baulks of timber that had once supported the crates of aircraft on deck. As he threw aside the wreckage and gained the deck, the ship gave another violent lurch. He was knocked off his feet and rolled across the deck towards the scuppers, crying out with pain as jagged metal cut into his bare feet and legs.

Fighting back rising panic, Bailey regained his feet and looked around him. He was alone on the after deck, surrounded by crumpled aircraft fuselages and smashed timbers. The ship was listing heavily to port and appeared to be settling rapidly in the water. His path to the boat deck, where he hoped the others were lowering the lifeboats – although he could hear no voices – was completely blocked by debris. Painfully, he clawed his way aft, planning to launch the liferaft stowed on the port side of the after masthouse. The raft was no longer there, blown clean away by the explosion of the torpedo.

Sick with disappointment and wracked by indecision, Bailey stood at the bulwark rail and gazed down into the sea, now only a few feet from the deck. Then the awful realization came that, in his fight to get clear of the accommodation, he had left his lifejacket behind. But there was no turning back. The

list was increasing and the water below becoming nearer with
every passing second. He climbed onto the bulwark rail and
prepared to jump. At that precise moment, the *Fort Mumford*
gave her dying lurch and began to roll over. Bailey lost his
grip and fell outwards.

Although the sea temperature was in the lower eighties,
to Bailey the water had the chill of death about it, as it closed
over him and he sank deep. He was frighteningly aware of
pieces of wreckage swirling around him and brushing against
his body. The ship was coming down on top of him and he
was sure the time had come for Horace Bailey to die. He let
his body go limp, but the instinctive will to survive would
not allow him to empty his lungs and finish it quickly.

When his lungs were on the point of bursting. Bailey suddenly found himself free of the wreckage and shooting upwards.
He surfaced near a large object similar in size and shape to
a liferaft. Kicking out, he swam towards it and dragged himself
aboard, finding himself on a flat hull section of one of the
landing craft once lashed to the deck of the *Fort Mumford.*
The craft would never see the beaches of Sicily, where it had
been destined to come ashore, but it might save the life of
Seaman Gunner Bailey.

Bailey's first move, having reached a place of refuge, was
to look around for other survivors. Balancing himself on his
makeshift liferaft, he searched the horizon, straining his eyes
to pierce the hazy darkness. The *Fort Mumford* had carried
a total crew of 53 and, although she had gone down in a few
minutes, it was inconceivable to Bailey that he could be the
only survivor. Yet he could see no movement on the water,
no red glow of lifejacket lights and – worst of all – no voices.
All around him there was only darkness and ominous silence.
His shoulders slumped and he sank to his knees.

After some ten minutes reflecting on the enormity of his
predicament, he heard a faint shout and his spirits soared.
Straightening up, he cupped his hands and shouted jubilantly
back across the water. There was no reply. He continued calling until he was hoarse, pleading with the other man – if there

was one – to answer. But there was only silence. Then he saw what looked like a small fire floating on the water in the direction he had heard the shout and he began calling again, certain he had seen a lifejacket light. Then the glow was gone and the lonely darkness once more closed in around him and he was again without hope. What Bailey had heard and seen can only be guessed at but the voice was almost certainly Japanese and the fire the flash of *I-27*'s exhaust as she motored quietly away from the scene of her night's work.

To Horace Bailey it seemed his life had sunk to its lowest ebb. The sinking of his ship – his home for more than three months – was a cruel enough blow. If the others had survived with him, and he knew now that none had, he could have drawn comfort from their presence, and with it hope. But to suffer in this empty ocean alone, to drift for days, perhaps weeks, with only the oblivion of death to look forward to, was a prospect that filled him with dread.

While he was reviewing the hopelessness of his predicament, Bailey noticed he had blood on his hands. For a moment he was puzzled, then he felt the pain and he remembered his fall on deck when the *Fort Mumford* had given her second violent lurch. Feeling with tentative fingers, he discovered deep lacerations to his legs and feet, presumably caused by nails or jagged metal in the wreckage of the deck cargo. One cut in his foot went almost to the bone and he was bleeding profusely.

A lesser man would have been tempted to lie down and wait for death, but Bailey, having come to terms with his plight, had ideas to the contrary. He cleaned his wounds with salt water and stopped the bleeding from the deep cut in his foot by plugging it with algae-like scrum scooped up from the surface of the sea. From then on, he knew his life depended on his own willpower and on the mercy of God, who had deemed that he alone should survive the sinking of the *Fort Mumford*.

For the next five days he drifted, clinging to the waterlogged side of the landing craft, his legs and back immersed in water for much of the time. He had no food, no water, no equipment, other than a small canvas ammunition box cover and a short length of timber he had rescued from the sea simply because they had floated near. There was hardly a breath of wind and during the day, the sun beat down on his half-naked body, burning his skin to a dark mahogany. Oddly enough, he felt no hunger but he suffered agonies from thirst. Shoals of small fish swam around and nuzzled at the edges of his raft and he made desperate efforts to catch one, hoping its raw flesh would help to assuage his terrible thirst. Eventually, his efforts were rewarded when he caught a fish by the tail and snatched it out of the water. By this time, he was so weak he was unable to kill the poor, struggling creature and he returned it to the sea.

At times he became feverish but it was his injured leg that caused him most concern, as it appeared to him to be growing thinner, almost withering before his eyes. It was perhaps this preoccupation with his leg that kept him sane. The turning point came on the fourth day, when an isolated shower of rain swept across the raft and Bailey was able to quench his thirst for the first time by licking the rain drops as they ran down his body. His spirits began to rise.

On the fifth day of his ordeal, he saw a white bird swooping low over the sea in the distance. For several minutes he watched, envying the bird's ability to skim over the waves. Then, as it rose above the horizon, the white bird became a sail and below the sail the hull of a small craft. With his hands trembling with excitement, Bailey snatched up the flotsam he had providentially collected. Working quickly, he tied the scrap of canvas to the broken plank and waved it above his head. Very soon, he found himself being handed gently over the bulwarks of a small dhow.

When his thirst had been slaked by a cup of water, he was given a concoction of eucalyptus oil and water, which seemed to act as a stimulant to his tired brain. His rescuers informed him he was on an Indian dhow bound from the Malabar Coast to Mikindani in Tanganyika. The dhow was of about 47 tons displacement and carried a crew of nine, who treated him with extreme kindness. On seeing the state of Bailey's injured foot, which had turned quite black, the sturdy brown men held him down and scrubbed the foot with boiling water. The agony Bailey went through was intense but there was no doubt the rough and ready Indian antisepsis saved his foot, for thereafter the wound began to heal cleanly.

Running before the prevailing northeasterly wind, which was light but steady, the dhow reached Mikindani on 7 May, forty-three days after Bailey had been picked up. The seaman gunner walked ashore in Tanganyika with only a slight limp to betray the terrible ordeal he had lived through. As to the men who saved his life, the only clue he had to their identity was the number of their small craft, 443.

The mystery of the disappearance of Captain John Henry Reardon Smith and the other 51 men of the *Fort Mumford* will probably never be unravelled. The ship was torpedoed at 8 o'clock in the night, when the watches were changing and very few of her crew would have been in their bunks. Although she sank quite quickly, it seems, as evidenced by Horace Bailey's actions until he was pitched overboard, there should have been ample time for many more men to get clear before the ship went down. It may be that some did survive and, like Bailey, drifted on makeshift rafts for days before dying of thirst and exposure. Wreckage identified as coming from the *Fort Mumford* was washed up on Cape Cormorin, 500 miles to the east of the sinking, but no bodies were ever found.

After the sinking of the *Fort Mumford*, Toshiaki Fukumura went from strength to strength, sinking in the following nine months 8 Allied ships totalling nearly 43,000 tons. His last act of war was to sink the British troopship *Khedive Ismail* near Addu Atoll on 12 February 1944. The British ship, which went down in two minutes, was carrying 1,947 passengers and crew, including British, American and African troops and members of the Women's services. More than 1,000 lives were lost. Retribution was, however, swift. *I-27* was herself sunk by the destroyers *Petard* and *Paladin*, which were escorting the troopship.

March 1943 had been a bad month for the ships of the Red Dragon. Evans and Reid's *Nailsea Court* and the Newport ship *Fort Lamy* had been lost in Convoy SC 121, the *Clarissa Radcliffe* had disappeared after straggling from Convoy SC 122, Tatem's *Hadleigh* had gone in the Mediterranean and the *Fort Mumford* in the Arabian Sea. Over 200 Welsh-based merchant seamen had given their lives while the yellow daffodils bloomed thick in the woodland glades of the land of Dewi Sant.

19

The St Essylt: operation husky

I t might truly be said the eighteen months spent in the Mediterranean by *U-375* up until June 1943 had not been an unqualified success. Under her commander Kapitän-Leutnant Jürgen Könenkamp, she had covered many thousands of miles and succeeded in sinking only two small ships, the 190-ton British armed trawler *Vassiliki* and a Palestinian coaster of 558 tons. She had also damaged the minelayer HMS *Manxman*, which Könenkamp erroneously claimed to be a London Class cruiser, and the British merchantman *Empire Kumasi* of 6,288 tons. It is true the *Empire Kumasi* was towed into Haifa and subsequently declared a total loss, but she could only be legitimately marked on *U-375*'s score sheet as 'damaged'. By July 1943, Könenkamp's prospects of amassing sufficient tonnage to qualify for his Knight's Cross seemed very poor indeed. However, an opportunity of increasing his rating, the like of which had never before been seen before by U-boat commanders, was about to come his way.

Some two weeks before Könenkamp had logged his first meagre sinking, the Casablanca Conference had agreed that the first large scale entry of Allied forces into Europe would be made through the island of Sicily. By the time the German and Italian forces in Tunisia had surrendered on 12 May, the invasion plans had been finalised and the date set for 9 July. Although it was known Sicily was inadequately defended, the planners had no wish to repeat the 1942 Dieppe fiasco, which itself had been a trial run for the invasion of Europe. Accordingly, the Sicily landings were planned on a massive and hopefully unstoppable scale. In Operation Husky, as the invasion was codenamed, a total of 2,700 ships carrying troops, armour and supplies were to be involved. In all, 34 separate convoys would set out from the United Kingdom, Malta and the Eastern Mediterranean, all converging on the island on the night of 9/10 July and on the days immediately following. The tideless sea would soon be covered in ships from horizon to horizon.

The *St Essylt*, a two-year-old motorship of 5,634 tons, owned by the South American Saint Line of Merthyr House Cardiff and registered in Newport Mon., had neither been designed nor built as a troopship. Nevertheless, in June 1943 she found herself in Glasgow taking on board in addition to 900 tons of military stores, over 300 men of the Canadian First Division. With her crew increased to 79 by the addition of an extra 12 DEMS gunners, the *St Essylt* left the Clyde for the beaches of Sicily with a total of 401 personnel on board. In her holds she carried military vehicles stowed on top of cases of ammunition and stores while the two landing craft destined to put her troops ashore were lashed on top of her No. 2 hatch. Her defensive armament consisted of a 4-inch anti-submarine gun, a Bofors 40 mm anti-aircraft gun, 8 Oerlikons, 2 twin Marlin machine guns and various anti-aircraft rockets.

At the Tail of the Bank, the *St Essylt*, commanded by Captain S. Diggins, formed up with the 17 other similarly loaded ships of Convoy KMS 18B and sailed from the Clyde on 24 June. It was no comfort to Captain Diggins to find his ship allotted the convoy number 17, rear ship of the port wing column and therefore in a most exposed position with regard to attack by U-boat. Nor was Diggins, in his almost-new motorship, happy with the designated speed of Convoy KMS 18B, a mere 8 knots. He was only too aware of the capabilities of the enemy's U-boats. The Type VII-C's had a maximum speed of 17.3 knots surfaced and 7.6 knots submerged and would have no difficulty in shadowing the convoy in order to attack when they had the best advantage. Then the *St Essylt*, on the perimeter and at the rear of the convoy, could be one of the first to come under attack.

But, at least as far as the Atlantic sector of his voyage was concerned, Diggins had little to fear from the U-boats. The increased use of radar-equipped aircraft by the Allies had resulted in the loss of 41 U-boats in the first three weeks in May and the pressure on the enemy was being kept up. It was rumoured Dönitz had now withdrawn the majority of his wolf-packs from the North Atlantic. It was not surprising then, that the convoy's eight-day passage from the Clyde to Gibraltar, via the north of Ireland, passed without incident. No U-boat warnings were received from the Admiralty, nor were hostile craft detected or sighted.

The second day of July saw KMS 18B steaming through the Straits of Gibraltar with the land in sight on both sides. The convoy then had just over 1,000 miles to cover to its appointment with the island of Sicily, which was already being softened up by saturation bombing by Allied aircraft. On 4 July, when American troops assembling for embarkation in the North African ports were indulging in a subdued celebration of their Independence Day, KMS 18B was closing the coast of Algeria, some 600 miles from its destination. All the ships were keeping Double British Summertime (GMT–2) so that, by the time the sun was setting astern of the convoy on that night, it was almost 21.00. In the twilight, the rocky promontary of Cape Tenez was just visible to the southeast at 25 miles.

The troops crowding the decks of the *St Essylt* looked longingly at the distant land, for the Mediterranean was hardly living up to their expectations. A fresh easterly wind had whipped up a short, rough sea, giving the ship an uncomfortable corkscrewing motion. For Jürgen Könenkamp, the agitation of the sea was a welcome asset, hiding the wake of his periscope as he brought *U-375* into a favourable position to commence his attack. His first torpedo hit the 8,762-ton British cargo vessel *City of Venice*, leading ship of the second column. She began to sink at once.

On the bridge of the *St Essylt*, Captain Diggins took

immediate steps to bring his ship into a state of readiness. Action stations was sounded on the alarm bells, all troops ordered out of the messdecks, extra lookouts posted and all guns manned. At the same time, for some reason beyond explanation, the convoy commodore signalled all ships to cease zigzagging and reduce speed to 7 knots. The effect of this action was to give Könenkamp a big advantage. He made full use of it.

At 21.45 the *St Essylt*, maintaining a steady course of 080° and moving through the water at only 7 knots, was hit by a torpedo in the starboard side of her No. 2 hold. It is hard to imagine how Könenkamp could have missed. The force of the explosion blew the beams and hatches off No. 2 hold, smashing and overturning the landing craft stowed on top of this hatch, Flames and smoke poured out of the hold, indicating that the vehicles stowed below had caught fire. The ship took on a heavy starboard list. Diggins, acting cooly and decisively, stopped his engines and ordered his wireless operator to transmit a message informing the convoy of the *St Essylt*'s plight.

Within minutes, it could be seen from the bridge that No. 2 hold had become an inferno, with flames shooting over 100 feet into the air. This quickly set alight the ammunition and petrol stowed on deck and abaft the burning hold and Diggins knew the time had come to think about the safety of the men consigned to his charge.

For her total complement of 401, the *St Essylt* carried her normal equipment of 4 lifeboats, supplemented by numerous liferafts and small floats. It was at once obvious to Diggins that, with so many men to get clear, the evacuation would take some time and, in order to avoid unnecessary loss of life, it must be carried out with the minimum of panic. He also decided he would remain with his ship so long as there was even the remotest possibility of saving her.

The signal to abandon ship was sounded and, directed by the *St Essylt*'s crew, the Canadian troops began to leave the burning ship. With the vessel listing heavily and exploding ammunition and drums of petrol adding to the horror, the evacuation took place calmly and relatively unhurriedly. Due largely to the tight discipline of the troops and the unruffled efficiency of their officers, all those leaving were off the ship 25 minutes after she had been hit.

It was not, however, all to go smoothly. The *St Essylt*'s 4 lifeboats were soon full and the majority of the survivors were forced to jump into the sea and take their chances with the rafts and floats. Those unfortunate enough to have only one of the small floats to cling to suffered harsh treatment at the hands of the rough sea and many clambered into the already overloaded lifeboats, sinking them to their gunwales. Panic broke out when those in the boats realized their danger, but order was soon restored and men redistributed on the rafts so that the waterlogged boats could be bailed out.

Still on the bridge of his blazing ship, Captain Diggins had gathered around him a small band of volunteers, who had offered to remain on board to clear away the rafts and floats and to assist in saving the ship, if this was at all possible. With Diggins were Chief Officer D. Robertson, Second Engineer R. Tucker, Sgt. G. W. Brown and L/Bdr G. A. Bassett of the R.A. Maritime Regiment, and Sgt. R. Hillcoat and Bdr. R. N. Ritchie of the Royal Canadian Army.

When the evacuation of the ship was complete, Diggins led his party forward with the object of making a closer assessment of the situation. Unfortunately a fresh series of explosions broke out as they made their way up the foredeck and flying debris and tracer bullets forced then to retire to the comparative safety of the poop deck. If the means had been available, Diggins would then have abandoned the ship altogether, but not even the smallest of floats remained to support them in the water. He decided to wait until rescue arrived.

At about 22.30, the corvette HMS *Honeysuckle* arrived on the scene and began picking up men out of the water around the *St Essylt*. In spite of the rough sea, *Honeysuckle*'s boat's crew did magnificent work, snatching the exhausted soldiers from the rafts and ferrying them to the corvette. *Honeysuckle* was soon joined by a second corvette, HMS *Rhododendron*, and the Navy tug HMS *Restive*.

Meanwhile, Captain Diggins and his six companions were crouched in the shelter of the *St Essylt*'s poop deckhouse. The explosions on the foredeck were merging into one continuous thunder and Diggins knew they must leave the ship soon, or go down with her. Reluctantly, he told Chief Officer Robertson to signal *Honeysuckle* with his torch, informing the corvette of their presence on board the burning ship. When *Honeysuckle* offered to close the ship and attempt to take them off, Diggins insisted she see to the men in the water first.

A few minutes later, an enormous bang was heard from the foredeck when a stack of ammunition boxes exploded as one. The whole fore part of the ship was now a sea of flame, which was creeping relentlessly aft. The situation being patently hopeless, Diggins instructed Robertson to signal *Honeysuckle* that they were about to abandon ship. Without hesitation and despite the billowing flames, the flying debris and the hail of exploding tracer bullets, the corvette began to close in. Handing his lifejacket to one of the Army men, who was unable to swim, Diggins led the way over the side.

In his battle with the sea, turned blood red by the flames from his doomed ship, Diggins lost touch with the others, but he was a strong swimmer and was very soon pulling himself up the corvette's scrambling net and calling for a boat. Once aboard *Honeysuckle*, he made straight for her bridge to advise on the possible location of those still in the water. When the six men who had bravely stood by with him on the *St Essylt* to the last had been picked up, Diggins, although by this time himself nearing exhaustion, remained on the bridge of the corvette assisting with the rescue operation.

By 02.00 on the 5th, *Honeysuckle* had taken 276 men alive from the sea and, with *Rhododendron* and *Restive*, continued the search throughout the night. At 05.45, when the task was nearing its end and Diggins had finally been persuaded to go below, the *St Essylt* blew up and sank. When Diggins reached the deck of the corvette, his ship had gone.

Honeysuckle broke off her search at 08.00 and set course for Algiers. In all, the rescue ships had picked up 397 survivors from the Welsh ship, the body of one of her stewards had been found and only 32 servicemen were missing. In view of the weather, the sheer number of men involved and the nature of the *St Essylt*'s cargo, her casualties were remarkably few. Much of the credit for this miracle must go to Captain Diggins, without whose cool, overall direction of the abandonment and subsequent involvement in the search for survivors, many more men would have died.

But there were many heroes on that night 4/5 July 1943 and Captain Diggins did not hesitate to name them.

> *Chief Officer D. Robertson*: 'This officer was outstanding in his efforts in getting the crew and troops clear of the burning ship. He unhesitatingly volunteered to remain on board with me in case anything could be done to save the ship, and was remarkably cool and efficient throughout.'
>
> *Chief Engineer W. Marrs*: 'Although the fore part of the ship was burning furiously, Mr Marrs went down into the engineroom to ascertain that all his staff were clear and also to stop pumps which were causing discharge likely to flood the lifeboats. He also did good work in maintaining discipline amongst the men in No. 3 lifeboat when that boat became waterlogged and he assisted in towing several of the rafts clear of the burning vessel.'
>
> *Second Engineer R. Tucker*: 'This officer volunteered to remain on board as long as he was required; he was the last but one to leave the vessel and throughout this trying ordeal was remarkably cool and calm.'
>
> *Able Seaman M. McNeil*: 'I consider that Able Seaman McNeil is a very fine sailor. When the forward fall of No. 3 lifeboat went with a run, he stopped it by means of a rope stopper. The forward fall was again accidentally cut, instead of the rope stopper but with great presence of mind, McNeil ran aft and cut the after fall, thereby allowing the boat to go down more or less on an even keel.'
>
> *Sgt. G. W. Brown and L/Bdr. G. A. Bassett, R.A. Maritime Regt.*: 'Both these men greatly assisted in getting men off the ship,

afterwards volunteering to remain on board with the Chief Officer and myself in case their services were required.'

Major Ware, P.P.C.L.I. OC Troops: 'Major Ware was very calm and efficient throughout, assisting in getting his men organized and away from the ship quickly and efficiently. When all his men were clear, he reported to me and asked if he could be of further assistance, but I ordered him to follow his men so he jumped overboard and swam to a raft.'

Lt. Merryweather, RNVR (S.N.O.T.): 'Lieutenant Merryweather was very calm and efficient and assisted in getting the men clear of the ship. He remained on board until ordered to abandon ship along with the OC Troops.'

Company Sgt. Major C. H. Blower (1021 Docks Operating Company, R.E.): 'Company Sgt. Major Blower did excellent work in assisting to get the troops into No. 3 lifeboat. He remained on board to assist in releasing the rafts long after his own boat had pulled away from the ship.'

Sgt. R. Hillcoat and Bdr. R.N. Ritchie, R.C.A.; 'These men greatly assisted in getting the troops clear of the ship and voluntarily remained on board with me in case their assistance was required.'

The landings on Sicily were a complete success, only 4 ships being lost out of the 2,700 involved in the operation. The fighting on the island lasted for thirty-nine days, an armistice being signed on 3 September. On that same day the Allies crossed the Straights of Messina to the mainland of Italy.

U-375's uninspiring record in the Mediterranean ended with the sinking of the *St Essylt*. Twenty-six days later, on 30 July, she was cornered and sunk off Pantelleria by the US patrol vessel *PC-624*. Jürgen Könenkamp went down with his boat.

20

The Cornish City: the U-cruisers

The Indian Ocean, first revealed to European eyes when Batholomew Diaz rounded the Cape of Good Hope in 1488, may be likened to a great oceanic bay bounded by the continents of Africa, Asia and Australasia. It covers an area of some 17 million square miles and plunges to nearly 23,000 feet at its deepest point. This vast sweep of blue water is troubled seasonally by the stormy Southwest Monsoon and sporadically by the rampaging cyclone, but being an area of permanent high pressure, its weather is in the main benign.

At Sunrise on 29 July 1943, the Indian Ocean eastwards of Madagascar was in one of its more playful moods. A brisk north-northeasterly breeze frothed the tops of a moderate swell but the weather was fine and clear, with eye-stretching visibility. A lone ship, the *Cornish City*, dipped her bows easily into the swell as she steamed steadily north making a shade under 10 knots. She was 240 miles off the coast of Madagascar and some 300 miles south of the island of Reunion, which she expected to pass at around noon on the following day.

On the bridge, Chief Officer K. E. Germaney, having finished his morning star sights, was enjoying the sunrise and reflecting on the quirk of fate which had brought about his sudden promotion from Second Officer to Chief Officer of the *Cornish City* less than two weeks before. His predecessor, injured in a shipboard accident, had been landed into hospital at Lourenco Marques in Mozambique and, overnight, Germaney found himself sewing on a third gold band and charged with, in addition to the 4 to 8 watch, the responsibility for

the whole of the deck operations of the ship. After the comparatively untaxing life he had enjoyed as ship's navigator and
keeper of the middle watch, the challenge posed by his changed
situation was somewhat daunting.

Captain Henry Isaac chose that moment to join Germaney
on the bridge. To Isaac, the sunrise over an empty and apparently friendly sea was yet another blessing to be counted. Having survived nearly four years of this bitter conflict at sea,
he was perhaps only too aware that he might be living on
borrowed time. But hope, like the sun on that clear morning,
was rising steadily. He had seen British shipping losses peak
at nearly 500,000 tons a month in the winter of 1942, then
fall off dramatically as the escorts gained superiority over the
U-boats. Crossing the North Atlantic was still no Sunday afternoon jaunt across the Bristol Channel – even in times of peace
it never would be – but for the merchant seaman the odds
in favour of survival had shortened considerably. Now, with
Italy on the verge of surrender, the Germans running out of
steam in Russia and the Americans beginning to flush the
Japanese out of the Pacific islands, it seemed possible the war
would soon be over. Isaac considered both he and the *Cornish
City* might, after all, live to see a return to the days when
men could again sail the seas without fear of death and destruction. Meanwhile, this Indian Ocean passage, with its unlike-
lihood of molestation, was a bonus to be savoured.

Isaac's confidence in the benignity of the Indian Ocean was
only partially justified. After the disappearance of the surface
raiders from the scene, the Axis striking power in the Ocean
was limited to a handful of German and Japanese U-boats,
among them still *U-182*, which had sunk Evan Thomas, Radcliffe & Co.'s *Llanashe* in February. Five of these boats, *U-172*,
U-177, *U-178*, *U-181* and *U-182*, had first rounded the Cape
in October of 1942. They had over the intervening months
wreaked considerable havoc amongst merchant shipping in
the Ocean, but they were now reaching the end of their endurance. At the beginning of May 1943, nine U-boats had set
out from the Biscay ports with the intention of relieving the

long-serving five but they had been so dogged by bad luck and harrassed by Allied aircraft, that they were unlikely to arrive before September, if at all. Informed of this situation, those awaiting relief had once again filled their bunker tanks from the supply ship *Charlotte Schliemann* to the south of Madagascar and gone their separate ways in search of new victims.

The *Cornish City* had not been away from her home port as long as the Indian Ocean U-boats, having left Cardiff in mid-February, loaded for South African ports. She was a 4,895-ton motorship built in 1936, one of the newer units in the fleet of Sir William Reardon Smith. Registered at Bideford, as were all Reardon Smith's ships, the Cornish City carried a crew of 43, including four young apprentices and six DEMS gunners. She was armed with the usual 12-pounder forward, a 4-inch aft, 4 twin-barreled machine guns on her bridge and 6 rocket launchers, sufficient for her to be able to put up a credible performance when attacked from the air or the surface of the sea. As was the case with all Allied merchant ships, she was completely defenceless against the submerged submarine.

The long sojourn on the South African coast, overflowing with the good things of life and lavish with open-hearted hospitality, had been sheer delight for Henry Isaac and his men. When the ship finally left Durban on the morning of 22 July, loaded with 9,600 tons of coal for Aden, they were ready to return to the realities of the war with good heart. Rolling to the ponderous swells outside the breakwaters of Durban, the *Cornish City* joined Convoy DN 53.

Compared with the huge 40-ship convoys of the North Atlantic, with their attendant destroyers, corvettes and occasional aircraft carrier, Convoy DN 53 was something of an anticlimax for Henry Isaac. This mini-convoy consisted of only five merchant ships, escorted by two enthusiastic but painfully ineffectual armed trawlers of the South African Navy. The only comfort Isaac was able to draw from the presence of the trawlers was that they were at least equipped with asdic and could give warning to the merchantmen of the approach of U-boats. Beyond that, there did not seem much point to the assembly. The main object of the convoy was, of course, to shepherd the heavily loaded merchant ships past the southern entrance to the Mozambique Channel, a hunting ground of long standing for German and Japanese U-boats. This was achieved by sunset on the 24th and it was with no misgivings that Isaac set the first of his independent courses for the Gulf of Aden and rang for full speed. From then on, he alone would control the destiny of his ship and his men. He was not to know this control was shortly to pass from his hands.

Korvetten-Kapitän Robert Gysae had, like Captain Henry Isaac, experienced all the horrors of the Battle of the Atlantic, albeit from the other side of the periscope. In *U-98*, he had sunk 10 ships, totalling 52,025 tons, over the period from March 1941 to February 1942, all the while enduring the rigours of the angry seas and suffering the frenzied onslaughts of the defending escorts. In October 1942 Gysae, in command of *U-177*, had entered the Indian Ocean in company with the other U-cruisers. Working his way across the Cape shipping lanes to the Mozambique Channel, the seasoned hunter had increased his score by nearly 72,000 tons. At the end of June, having taken fuel and supplies from the *Charlotte Schliemann*, he decided to cast his net to the east of Madagascar.

The 29th of July was just another day in the life of the *Cornish City*, the normal routine of shipboard life proceeding as it had from the day she left the shipyard. War, or no war, there were decks to be cleaned, cargo gear to overhaul, creeping rust to be attended to. At 09.35, with breakfast out of the way, Captain Isaac and Chief Officer Germaney walked the port wing of the lower bridge discussing priorities and programmes. With the warm sun shining down out of a blue sky dotted with cotton wool-like cumulus and the horizon as empty as a Welsh pub on a Sunday, it was a good day for making plans. Neither man saw the track of *U-177*'s torpedo racing in on the port side.

Gysae had aimed with precision and achieved the desired result. His torpedo struck the unsuspecting merchant ship in the vicinity of the watertight bulkhead between her engineroom and No. 4 hold. Deafened by the explosion, his nostrils filled with the stench of burnt cordite, Chief Officer Germaney watched in horror as the port side of the boat deck erupted in a great sheet of flame, which soared 150 feet in the air, taking the shattered remains of a lifeboat with it.

Her engineroom and adjacent hold flooding, the *Cornish City* began to sink at once, going down by the stern. Realizing there was little time left, Germaney hurried to the starboard side of the boat deck. Some of the crew were there before him and had lowered the lifeboat to the water, where it rose and fell on the waves, still made fast to the ship by its painter. Germaney looked aft to where the sea was now washing over the deck. As he did so, the *Cornish City* gave a violent shudder. Captain Isaac, who was now on the starboard side of the lower bridge, shouted a warning. Seconds later, Germaney saw the bows rear up in the air, while the deck he was standing on remained level. The *Cornish City* had broken her back.

Controlling his panic, Germaney slipped his lifejacket over his head. He had just time to tie one of the tapes of the bulky jacket, when the ship began to sink beneath him. As he went under, he saw the starboard lifeboat, still made fast to the ship by its 3-inch rope painter, dragged back on board into the maelstrom created by the sinking ship. There were already six men in the boat, their faces white, their mouths gaping open as the awfulness of their fate dawned on them.

Buoyed up by his lifejacket, Germaney came to the surface quickly. When he did, he found his ship and the lifeboat had gone. The wounding, the death and the burial of the *Cornish City* had taken no more than two minutes. After about half an hour in the water, with his mind running the gamut of fear, panic and despair, Germaney could hardly believe his luck when he sighted the liferaft with its two occupants. He was hauled on board, where he found himself in the company of the *Cornish City*'s Estonian born boatswain Grant and Fifth Engineer Plewes. The raft was one of the new DAB-type, which the *Cornish City* had only recently been equipped with. It was a substantial wooden craft of about 10 feet by 6 feet, having a shaped bow and stern and a drop keel.

As he lay on the deck of the raft gasping out his thanks to his rescuers, Germaney saw the submarine surfacing close by. His immediate reaction was to struggle out of his sodden uniform jacket with its tell-tale gold bands. He would rather take his chance with the sea than become a prisoner of the men who had sunk his ship.

The submarine, which was painted with an effective camouflage of alternate light and dark grey stripes and armed with a deck gun and anti-aircraft cannon at the after end of her conning tower, motored cautiously up to the raft. She carried no identification marks and flew no ensign but Germaney concluded she was a German U-boat. The conning tower was manned by six men, two whose high-crowned caps marked them as officers, and four lookouts, who constantly scanned the sky and horizon through binoculars. Even in this remote part of the ocean the U-boat men were not relaxing their guard.

When the raft bumped alongside the casing of the submarine, the older of the two officers, a big man with dark hair and a beard, who Germaney assumed to be the commander, leaned over the conning tower and addressed the survivors in English. Korvetten-Kapitän Gysae's questions were predictable and to the point. He required to know the name of the ship he had sunk, her port of registry, last port of call, her destination and cargo.

Germaney took it upon himself to be spokesman. Being in the hopeless position he was, it would have been understandable and excusable if he had let his tongue run riot, but he did nothing of the sort. He gave the name of his ship and, as the sea around him was covered in coal and dust, divulged the nature of the *Cornish City*'s cargo and would not be drawn further. Gysae continued with the one-sided interrogation for some time but, meeting a blank wall, eventually gave up in disgust. Germaney asked him for cigarettes but this request Gysae refused, possibly in retaliation for the lack of co-operation shown by the survivors. He did, however, wish them good luck and promised to send a wireless message reporting their position. With a quick wave, Gysae then backed *U-177* away from the raft and made off on the surface, heading in a west-northwesterly direction.

During his questioning by Gysae, Germaney had sighted another smaller raft, with three men aboard, drifting about 200 yards off. As soon as the U-boat was out of sight, he succeeded in bringing the two rafts together and found the three other survivors to be Apprentice E. Hall, Ordinary Seaman Millard and a DEMS gunner, Able Seaman W. E. Fletcher. Together with Germaney, Grant and Pewes, they were all that remained of the *Cornish City*'s crew of 43.

Germaney took command of the little band of survivors, transferring the newcomers to his own raft, which was better equipped and had ample space for six men. The provisions and water were taken from the smaller raft, which was then set adrift. Later that day, the men came across another DAB raft, which seemed to have come to the surface after their ship had gone down. The two large rafts were lashed together and, after taking an inventory, Germaney estimated that, with care, they had sufficient water, milk tablets, chocolate and biscuits to last them for 100 days. The rafts also had sails, canvas spray screens, sea anchors and smoke floats. He concluded their chances of survival were excellent, providing they were not unfortunate enough to be caught by a cyclone. The nearest land, Madagascar, lay some 250 miles to the west, but before attempting to set sail, Germaney decided it would be prudent to remain in the vicinity of the sinking for twenty-four hours in case a search for them was being made.

During the rest of that day, as the two tethered rafts, with their sea anchors streamed, drifted, the survivors swapped experiences. Following the torpedoing of the ship, their individual escapes had been narrow, but none more so than that of Fifth Engineer Plewes. The explosion had trapped him in his cabin and he had attempted to escape onto the deck through the porthole, which overlooked an outboard alleyway. The opening was a fraction too small for his hips and he ended up jammed in the porthole, able to move neither in nor out. Fortunately for him, help came in the form of Assistant Engineer Norman Bradley, who came down the alleyway at a run, heading for the after deck with the intention of jumping overboard. Bradley stopped to help Plewes out of the porthole and the two men went over the side together. Norman Bradley was never seen again.

Seaman Gunner Fletcher, without thought for his own safety, had rushed aft to the 4-inch gun when the torpedo struck. Although he was alone and the gun deck awash, he loaded the gun and trained it on the conning tower of the U-boat, which was above the water. Before he was able to fire, the ship sank under him and he was washed into the sea. In Fletcher's opinion, given another 30 seconds at the gun and *U-177* would have joined the *Cornish City* in her plunge to the bottom.

The night of the 29th was long but the survivors were comfortable and in good heart. Next morning, they breakfasted well on their emergency rations and settled down to discuss the possibility of sailing to Madagascar. At 11.30, as they were about to make sail, they sighted an aircraft low down on the southern horizon. As the plane drew nearer on what appeared to be a deliberate search pattern, it became recognizable as a Catalina flying boat.

Germaney tried to set off a smoke float but this stubbornly refused to ignite. The others, fearful that the plane might pass by without seeing them, tore down the raft's orange canvas screens and waved them frantically over their heads. Unlike the smoke float, this signal worked. The Catalina, which was about five miles off, banked and flew directly over them.

For the next three and a half hours the flying boat circled the rafts. A package was dropped which landed too far away for the survivors to retrieve but later the plane followed up with a tin of cigarettes tied to an inflated Mae West. This was recovered and the delighted seaman found inside the tin a note informing them that the navy was on the way.

At about 15.00, the Catalina gave one final dip of its wings and flew off. Once more alone on the empty ocean, the morale of the six men plummeted. But Germaney was equal to the change of mood, organizing the men into watches and thereby alleviating some of their feeling of helplessness. He saved the most punishing watch, midnight to 04.00, for himself. At about 03.20 on the morning of the 31st, when Germaney himself was in low spirits due to the melancholia of the small hours, he saw a flashing light reflecting on the clouds.

Jerking himself wide awake, he studied the flashes closely and was able to make out the morse letters VE, a code signal used by the Royal Navy for calling merchant ships. He was at first wary of answering the signal, fearing the U-boat might still be in the vicinity. But the flashing persisted, the lamp searching around the horizon, and he could no longer resist lighting the flare he had ready in his hand. Shortly before 05.00 the British destroyer HMS *Denizan* closed the rafts and the survivors were taken on board.

The men were landed at Port Louis, Mauritius, on 1 August, tired but none the worse for their experience. On arrival, Germaney was told their prompt rescue had been due to a wireless message giving their position, which had been picked up by Colombo Radio. The source of the message was unknown but, as no distress had gone out from the *Cornish City* before she sank, Germaney knew Robert Gysae had kept his promise.

Nothing was ever heard of the 36 men missing with the *Cornish City* and it must be assumed they went down with the ship. With them went Captain Henry Thomas Isaac of Barry, whose long war against the U-boats had at last come to an end.

U-177, last seen by Germaney heading to the west-northwest, sank the 4,195-ton Greek steamer *Efthalia Mari* five days later, but that was to be her last victory. In February 1944, when fruitlessly scouring the South Atlantic for targets, *U-177* was destroyed by an American Liberator on patrol from Ascension Island. Robert Gysae survived the sinking, and the rest of the war, later to become a Fleet-Admiral in Germany's new Navy.

21

The St Usk: the old ones die hard

By the late summer of 1943, the North Atlantic was rapidly returning to its normal role of being no more than an ocean perpetually troubled by the in-fighting of the warm and cold air masses which clash over its deep waters. After the massacre of the U-boats in May, when more than forty failed to return to their bases, it appeared Admiral Dönitz had at last accepted defeat in the West. In August, only 6 U-boats remained at large in the Atlantic, sinking in that month just 4 Allied merchant ships of 21,749 tons.

In September, however, Dönitz decided to make one more bid to cut Britain's Atlantic arteries, through which were flowing the lifeblood for the coming invasion of Europe. A force of 28 U-boats, including the 'milch cow' *U-460*, was despatched westwards from the Biscay bases. With them went *U-161*, commanded by Kapitän-Leutnant Albrecht Achilles. On his previous Atlantic patrol, in the spring of 1943, Achilles had suffered the gross humiliation of sinking only one ship – and that the Canadian sailing vessel *Angelus* of 255 tons. Achilles, determined to avoid a repeat of this fiasco, headed for the Brazilian coast, where potential targets did not enjoy the massive sea and air protection now provided for their North Atlantic counterparts.

Some three months earlier, the South American Saint Line's *St Usk* had loaded in London and slipped down Channel bound for her peacetime trading grounds, the east coast of South America. To say the *St Usk* was long in the tooth would be an understatement. She had, in fact, been built in 1909, at a time when the last of the great windjammers were still beating their way around the Horn. Having survived the Great War and twenty-one years of the gruelling tramp round, the *St Usk* was well past pensionable age and in the fourth year of her second war. Her record of service spoke for itself.

Commanded by Captain G. H. Moss, the 5,472-ton *St Usk* was a tall-masted, five hatch, single screw steamer capable, for all her great age, of a cruising speed of 9 knots. She carried a crew of 48, including 6 DEMS gunners, and was armed with a 12-pounder gun mounted on her forecastle head, a 4-inch aft, 4 Oerlikons and 2 twin Marlins. On her outward voyage, in convoy to Freetown and then unescorted across the South Atlantic, these accoutrements of war had seemed singularly unnecessary. Begun in a London made grey and lifeless by the privations of the long conflict, every day of the 28-day passage had been seen by Captain Moss and his crew as a step further into the beckoning sunrise. Throughout, the weather had been fine, the sea in a gentle mood and the enemy conspicuous by his absence. Then, at the end of the long trip there had been Brazil, a lush, green land with frightening extremes of poverty and wealth but so far removed from the war as to resemble another planet. Two months of this unreal paradise had been enough for the men of the *St Usk*. When the time came to go home, they were ready.

The harbour of Rio de Janeiro is said to be the most beautiful in the world. Surrounded by massive, forest-clad mountains, it is certainly one of the most impressive. It is also the largest natural, deep-water harbour in the world, capable of sheltering a vast number of ocean-going ships at any one time. At five o'clock in the afternoon of 15 September 1943, with only an hour of daylight left, the *St Usk* sailed from this great harbour loaded with 6,500 tons of general cargo. She was to proceed independently to Freetown and there join a convoy for the United Kingdom, back-tracking exactly on her outward passage in the early summer. Her course to Sierra Leone lay directly across the old sailing ship routes to and from the Horn, passing mid-way between St Pauls Rocks and Ascension Island. At her estimated speed of 9 knots, the passage was expected to take eighteen days, with the Southeast Trades blowing abaft her starboard beam for much of the time. According to information received by Captain Moss before sailing, there were no U-boats known to be operating in the area his ship would cross.

Forty-eight hours out into the Atlantic, on the 17th, warning was received from the Admiralty of the presence of a U-boat in the *St Usk*'s path and a diversion was recommended and made. Captain Moss also took the precaution of posting extra lookouts. Two or more days passed without incident until, at 17.10 on the evening of the 19th, a heavy shock was felt by those at the after end of the ship. Below decks in the engine-room, the bump was sufficient to throw the lubricating oil out of the thrust-block oil well of the propellor shaft, indicating to the engineer on watch that the ship had struck a sizeable object.

On the bridge, some forty feet above the waterline, Chief Officer E. C. Martyn, who had the 4 to 8 watch, felt nothing. Had he done so, he might well have concluded the ship had been in contact with a whale, a not uncommon happening in these waters. However, Martyn's peace was soon disturbed by the jangling of the after telephone bell. Picking up the receiver, he heard the breathless voice of the DEMS gunner on watch on the 4-inch gun platform reporting the bump and adding the disturbing news that a periscope was visible twenty yards off the port quarter and overtaking the ship. Martyn ordered the helm hard to starboard to sheer the ship away from the danger and called the captain to the bridge.

The periscope was no longer visible when Captain Moss arrived on the bridge a minute or so later. On being briefed on the happenings, he set the ship zig-zagging and called for the carpenter to sound all bilges to ascertain if the hull had been breached in the supposed collision. The results of the soundings proved negative and left Moss with a puzzle on his hands. The shock felt on the after deck and in the engine-room had not been imagined but could conceivably be put down to a basking whale, or even a sunken ship floating just below the surface – there were many such derelicts drifting around the oceans in those days of violence at sea. However, the gunner was adamant that he had seen a periscope. Could it be a U-boat had been shadowing them and the two ships, one above and one below the water, had inadvertently collided? Nothing more was seen and, after dark, Moss discontinued the zig-zag, anxious to be clear of the spot as soon as possible.

At twenty-three minutes before midnight, Third Officer R. H. Russel called Moss to the bridge, reporting having felt two heavy bumps forward, with an interval of two or three minutes between them. He described them as 'powerful, muffled thuds' and his description was confirmed by crew members, whose accommodation was under the forecastle head. Nothing was sighted by the lookouts.

There was now no doubt in Moss's mind that they were being shadowed by a submarine – and a particularly clumsy one at that. But he still could not be sure and was reluctant to order the sending of the emergency SSS message, indicating he was under attack by submarine. In any case, there was a dearth of Allied naval ships in this area and any plea for help was unlikely to be answered. Moss decided to carry on and hope for the best.

Chief Officer Martyn heard the news of the night's incident when he took up his watch at 04.00 on the 20th. The *St Usk* had now moved a further forty miles to the northeast without trouble and it seemed possible she had escaped the danger. The U-boat – if there indeed was one – had presumably been in contact for seven hours but, as far as was known, no torpedo had been fired at the ship. Had the U-boat perhaps been damaged in the collision? There were a dozen puzzling questions and an equal number of inconclusive answers.

The sun came up on the 20th into a fine, cloudless sky. A moderate sea was running, urged on by an east-southeasterly wind of force 5 blowing just forward of the *St Usk*'s starboard beam. It was a pleasant, fresh South Atlantic morning with the promise of a warm day to come. Martyn's star sights, taken at dawn, had fixed the ship's position as 290 miles north of Ilha da Trinidade, a tiny dot in the ocean, once used as a departure point by sailing ships bound around the Cape of Good Hope for Australia.

At 06.50, the *St Usk* was on a course of 038° and making 9 knots when Albrecht Achilles gave the order to fire. Seconds later Martyn, who was pacing the port wing of the bridge, felt the ship stagger under him and heard a muffled explosion from aft. He swung quickly around to see a tall column of water erupting from the port side of No. 5 hold. With the water went the tarpaulins and hatchboards of both after holds, while the heavy wooden main-topmast slowly leaned over and crashed to the deck, bringing with it a tangled mess of rigging, halyards and aerials. The sudden violent racing of the *St Usk*'s engines, indicating her propellor had gone, added to the confusion of the moment.

Captain Moss reached the bridge to find his ship in her death throes, the waves already lapping over her after deck as she settled by the stern. By some miracle, only one man had been injured by the explosion, a DEMS gunner who was trapped below decks with a sprained ankle and slight head injuries. While efforts were being made to extricate this man, Moss ordered an emergency wireless aerial rigged so that an SOS might be sent out. Unfortunately, although the aerial was rigged, no transmission could be made. As had so often happened in the torpedoing of a merchant ship, the delicate valves of the *St Usk*'s transmitter had been smashed by the explosion.

Although the ship had only a slight list to port and her rate of sinking had slowed, Moss realized the situation was hopeless and did not hesitate to order his men to abandon ship. Both lifeboats were lowered without difficulty, care being taken to stow the portable lifeboat transmitter in the starboard boat before lowering. As an added precaution, all four liferafts were also launched. Less than fifteen minutes following the torpedoing, all hands were in the lifeboats and pulling away from the ship, the after deck of which was now awash to the height of the 4-inch gun platform.

The *St Usk*, having survived the perils of the sea for thirty-four years, did not die easily. It was at 07.50, exactly one hour after she had been so cruelly wounded, that the old ship finally gave up the fight and slid beneath the waves. Her late crew, who were at work transferring stores from the surplus liferafts into the boats, broke off and watched in silence as she went. The transfer of the stores had just been completed when Martyn, in charge of No. 1 lifeboat, saw the submarine come to the surface and head towards his boat.

The sleek light grey hull was about 280 feet long and Martyn judged the U-boat to be of the largest type of around 1,200 tons. On the fore part of her conning tower was painted a Viking ship on a shield and alongside that the outline of a submarine cancelled by a white cross, probably indicating the U-boat had sunk an Allied submarine. Martyn took careful note of her guns, an 88 mm on the fore casing and 6 Oerlikon-type light anti-aircraft guns mounted around the conning tower.

Figures in uniform now appeared in the conning tower and Martyn instinctively shrank back as one of them raised his binoculars and began to study his boat. The commander was probably looking for potential prisoners, the master of the *St Usk* and one or two senior officers, perhaps. After a few minutes the man lowered his glasses and the U-boat moved off towards the other lifeboat, leaving Martyn to heave a sigh of relief. Uninviting though his present predicament might be, he had no wish to spend the rest of the war in a German prisoner of war camp.

U-161 closed No. 2 lifeboat, where her crew, all young, fit and sunburned, began to hand out mugs of coffee to the survivors. Martyn licked his lips and edged his own boat closer. He watched anxiously as the *St Usk*'s Second Officer, B. J. Derry, was taken aboard the U-boat. He was closely followed by Captain Moss and Third Radio Officer V. J. Mason. Martyn later learned that the two younger officers were taken because Moss, who had prudently removed all signs of his rank, had refused to identify himself as the ship's captain when challenged.

The U-boat commander then signalled Martyn to bring his boat alongside. This the chief officer did with reluctance and was not surprised when, having tied up the lifeboat to the submarine's casing, he was also ordered on board.

To Martyn, Kapitän-Leutnant Albrecht Achilles appeared a neat, courteous man in his early thirties. He wore a tropical rig of khaki jacket and shorts with weather-faded epaulettes, which might have once been of gold or silver lace. His English was excellent, with little trace of an accent.

It soon became obvious that Martyn was not to join the other prisoners, for Achilles gave him an approximate position and a course to steer for the nearest Brazilian port, Bahia, some 500 miles to the west. He suggested the lifeboats would make about fifty miles a day and inquired if the chief officer needed anything to help with the journey. Martyn asked only for medical attention for the injured gunner and more drinking water. Both these requests were granted without question, the gunner receiving attention from the U-boat's doctor and three tins of water being passed down to the boats.

Encouraged by the helpful attitude of the commander, Martyn now questioned Achilles about the mysterious bumps felt aboard the *St Usk* on the night of 19th. Achilles denied being in collision with the ship but did admit to firing two torpedoes at her that night, one which had missed astern and the other passing ahead of the ship. Martyn gathered the impression that Achilles had fired rather more than two torpedoes but was reluctant to admit so. The mystery of the night of the 19th was not solved, but it seems likely the bumps felt could have been *U-161*'s torpedoes hitting the ship and failing to explode.

While Martyn and Achilles were in conversation, one of the U-boat's crew was seen removing the portable wireless transmitter from the lifeboat. Martyn protested strongly but Achilles, while expressing regret, pointed out that he could not afford to have his position given away. Martyn could not deny the sense of this and, mindful of the kindness already shown by the commander, made no further protest.

As there now seemed no point in delaying the inevitable, Martyn made ready to return to his boat. Before leaving, he shook hands with Captain Moss and his two fellow prisoners, asking if they had any messages he could take home for them, assuming he would survive the long, hazardous journey ahead of him. At this point, Captain Moss disclosed his identity to Achilles and asked him to release the young officers taken with him. Achilles, having achieved his object, agreed and Derry and Mason, looking suitably relieved, joined the others in the boats. Before being taken down the conning tower hatch, Moss wrote a short note to his wife and handed it to Martyn. With a lump in his throat, Martyn again shook his captain's hand and jumped down into the boat. *U-161*'s diesels then roared into life and she moved off, heading in a southerly direction.

At 10.45, the two lifeboats hoisted their sails and set off together, running before the fresh east-southeasterly breeze. Martyn's boat carried twenty men while the other boat, in charge of Second Officer Derry, had twenty-seven. During the night the boats lost contact with each other and, by daylight on the 21st, Martyn found his boat was alone. Thinking the other boat, carrying more weight, had fallen astern, he lowered his sails and waited. After some hours, with nothing showing on the horizon, he decided to press on for the land.

For the first five days, the boat made good progress. The wind was steady, the weather perfect, with the days not too hot and the nights not too cold. An awning, made up of boat covers and canvas screens taken from the rafts, was rigged and, with an ample supply of water and provisions, the survivors were as comfortable as they could be under the circumstances.

At 08.00 on Sunday 26 September, after sailing steadily west-northwest for six days, a high-flying aircraft was sighted. Smoke floats were hurriedly set off but, to the great disappointment of Martyn and his fellow survivors, the aircraft passed overhead apparently without having seen them. Hope returned in the early afternoon, when another aircraft came in low and began to circle the boat. The aircraft, a United States patrol plane, dropped tins of food and a message advising the survivors a ship was coming to their rescue, adding that the *St Usk*'s other lifeboat had already been picked up. The pilot of the aircraft also gave Martyn a position. The lifeboat was only 130 miles to the southeast of Bahia.

It all seemed cut and dried. After six days of not unduly arduous sailing, rescue was at hand. But things began to go wrong. For the next twenty-six hours, the men searched the horizon in vain. Not a wisp of smoke or a mast was sighted. Then, just after 16.00 on the afternoon of the 27th, when all hope was fading, an aircraft with Brazilian markings appeared and twice circled the lifeboat before flying off to the south. Apart from a wave of the hand from the pilot, there was no communication, but Martyn was confident help must be very close. Again he was disappointed.

Night came and the weather deteriorated, the wind rising to gale force and heaping up a dangerous sea. This continued for the next twenty-four hours and, although the men were wet and miserable, the boat sailed well, Martyn keeping it always before the wind. By daybreak on the 29th, the weather was easing and the low Brazilian coast in sight ahead.

Martyn now had no idea of his position and turned the boat to sail parallel to the coast, looking for signs of civilisation. Some hours later, he sighted a lighthouse and a few isolated houses. At the same time, a small Brazilian ship was seen but, although smoke floats were burned and rockets fired from the lifeboat, the ship passed by. Being by now hardened to false hopes, Martyn decided to close the coast and attempt to land. As he turned the boat in for the lighthouse, the ship suddenly reversed her course and steamed towards them.

Their rescuer, the Brazilian ship *Porta Segua*, towed them into an anchorage close by the lighthouse, which proved to be some thirty miles to the south of Bahia. The survivors spent the night on board the *Porta Segua*, the master obliging Martyn by sending a cable to the British Consul at Bahia. Next afternoon, the survivors reboarded their lifeboat and were towed to Bahia by a local schooner.

At 13.00 on the 30th, after having sailed a distance of some 750 miles in nine days twelve hours, Martyn and his nineteen companions stepped ashore on Brazilian soil. They later heard that the other twenty-seven men of their crew had been picked up by the Spanish ship *Al Bareda* on the 25th and landed at Rio de Janeiro, from whence the *St Usk* had originally set sail ten days earlier.

U-161 claimed only one more victim after the *St Usk*, sinking on the 26 September the 4,998-ton Brazilian steamer *Itapage*. Twenty-four hours later, and only 100 miles to the north of where Martyn's lifeboat was then being circled by a Brazilian aircraft, *U-161* was herself sunk by a US Navy Catalina. Kapitän-Leutnant Albrecht Achilles and Captain G. H. Moss, captor and captive, found a common grave together in the cold depths of the South Atlantic.

22

The Newton Pine and the Sarastone: the dragon breathes fire

During the course of a voyage, be it long or short, the merchant seaman inevitably becomes deeply attached to his ship, no matter how old and ugly she may be, for she is both his livelihood and his temporary home. Let someone try to take her from him and he will breathe fire, as does the dragon.

Throughout the long war at sea, it was only on rare occasions the British merchant ship was able to make use of her limited armament against a visible enemy. All too often, the attack took place in the dead of the night and the crash of the torpedo, quickly followed by the flooding water, was the first and only indication of danger. Usually, it was then too late for anything but the hurried scramble for the boats and the rafts. When given the opportunity to take up arms in their defence, merchant seamen did so with a remarkable efficiency, born out of desperation and anger. The men of the Welsh ships were no exception.

The 4,212-ton steamship *Newton Pine*, owned by the Graig Shipping Company and registered in Cardiff, left Buenos Aires on 27 November 1940 bound for Freetown. She was loaded with 1,134 tons of wheat and barley consigned to a British port. Built in 1925, the *Newton Pine* carried a crew of 37 and was armed with a 12-pounder forward and a 4-inch gun aft, both sad reminders of a war fought twenty-two years before. In command was Captain C. N. Woolner, a master mariner not to be trifled with – as indeed were most of his breed.

On the passage to Freetown, the ship sailed unescorted and following the recommended Admiralty route given to Captain

Woolner by the British Consul in Buenos Aires. As she progressed across the broad, unruffled acres of the South Atlantic, the war seemed like a fading nightmare, yet far to the north, Convoy HX 90 was making its way slowly eastwards through the storms and into the U-boat trap that would all but destroy it. Woolner was also not privy to the knowledge that, after savaging Convoy HX 84, the *Admiral Scheer* had moved southwards, sinking the steamer *Port Hobart* off Bermuda on the 24th. Had he known of these events in the north, it is doubtful if his equilibrium would have been seriously disturbed, for his ship was but a very small dot on a vast ocean. However, Woolner was not naïve enough to drop his guard altogether, as evidenced by the frequent gun drills and practice shoots he carried out on the passage.

The Equator was crossed in the early hours of the morning of 13 December and by noon that day the *Newton Pine* was only three days steaming from Freetown. The weather was idyllic, with a light easterly wind and the sea disturbed only by the ship's wake as she zig-zagged her way to the northeast. At ten minutes before four, the Second Officer, nearing the end of his four-hour watch on the bridge, saw a torpedo break the surface at about 1,500 yards off the starboard quarter. Acting instinctively, he ordered the helm hard to port, swinging the ship away from the track of the torpedo. Pausing only to throw the switch on the alarm bells, he ran back out to the starboard wing of the bridge in time to watch the torpedo, clearly visible in the clear water, pass along the ship's side at no more than 15 feet from her plates.

Captain Woolner arrived on the bridge quickly and was witness to the wasted torpedo porpoising across the bow 1,500 yards ahead of the ship. Without hesitation, he brought the *Newton Pine* around onto a course of 315°, putting her, as far as he could judge, stern-on to the direction from which the torpedo had come. There was no sign of the attacking submarine.

Half an hour later, when Woolner and his chief officer were together in the chartroom, composing a wireless message to be sent to warn all ships of the presence of a submarine in the area, the sound of gunfire was heard. Both men rushed out onto the bridge to see shells bursting in the water astern of the ship. On the surface, between four and five miles off the port quarter, was the long, sleek outline of a submarine, her forward gun spitting flame.

Altering course to put the submarine directly astern, Woolner ordered the 4-inch gun's crew, who were already at their station, to open fire. The battle for survival was on. Manoeuvring his ship to present always the smallest possible target to his attacker, Woolner directed the fire of the 4-inch from the bridge. The *Newton Pine*'s first shell fell short and to the left, her second in line with the submarine but still short. Woolner increased the range and deflection and the third shot landed very close to the enemy.

The *Newton Pine* was now steaming at her maximum speed of 9 knots, with the submarine's shells falling anything up to 100 yards short of her squat stern. It soon became evident, however, that the submarine was rapidly overtaking the fleeing ship and, as the distance shortened, the shots crept nearer, until they were bursting only fifty yards astern. Soon the ship was being straddled by shells, apparently fired by two guns simultaneously.

The submarine was now close enough for Woolner to get a good look at her. To him she appeared to be an Italian, although he could see no ensign or markings. She had an exceptionally long conning tower, square-cut at its fore end, with the two guns now firing mounted immediately forward of the tower.

Crouched behind their unprotected 4-inch, the *Newton Pine*'s after gun's crew were in their stride and putting to good effect the lessons learned in the regular gun drills on the passage north. Their shells were falling close to and directly ahead of the pursuing submarine, which was from time to time disappearing from sight behind fountains of water thrown up by the British shells.

Captain Woolner, his knuckles showing white as he gripped the after rail of the bridge, knew it could only be a matter of time before his ship was overcome by the superior firepower of the enemy. When a shell exploded only ten feet off the ship's side abreast the after hatch, he decided drastic evasive action was called for. Ordering the 4-inch to cease fire, he put the helm hard to starboard and swing the ship's head through 60 degrees, putting the submarine on his starboard quarter. This move, he hoped, would confuse the enemy's aim and also give his own gun's crew a clearer view of their target.

The ploy worked. The submarine's shells began to overshoot the *Newton Pine*, landing between 50 and 150 yards off her port bow. Woolner ordered the 4-inch to recommence firing and, to his great satisfaction, the first shell from the gun scored a hit on the submarine's waterline, nearly blotting her out in a great cloud of smoke and spray. The second shell exploded immediately in front of the conning tower. The submarine ceased firing and rolled heavily to one side, almost submerging her conning tower. She then straightened up with only the upper part of the conning tower visible above the water then, a few seconds later, she was gone. The *Newton Pine*'s masthead lookout reported seeing her half-surface two or three times before finally disappearing from sight.

Woolner, uncertain as to whether his adversary had sunk or merely submerged to make a torpedo attack, ordered a smoke float dropped astern. When the black, oily smoke had formed a thick screen between him and the submarine's position, he steamed off to the northwest at full speed. A good lookout was kept for the submarine during the rest of daylight and throughout the night but it did not reappear.

Altogether, the action had lasted no more than thirty minutes, during which the *Newton Pine* fired 22 rounds from her 4-inch while, in Woolner's estimation, the submarine had fired 50 to 60 shells. The merchant ship had suffered no damage or casualties, although there had been a near-disaster in her galley. In the excitement of the fight, the *Newton Pine*'s cook, who had taken it upon himself to carry buckets of tea to the thirsty gun's crews, unfortunately overlooked the batch of bread he had in the galley oven. Only the timely disappearance of the submarine saved the loaves from burning and the cook from the wrath of Captain Woolner.

The identity and ultimate fate of the submarine which attacked the *Newton Pine* never came to light, but it is possible she was the Italian submarine *Foca*, reported lost in the Mediterranean on an unspecified day in December 1940. It may well be the *Foca* ventured out into the South Atlantic and met her end at the hands of Captain Woolner's gunners.

The gallant *Newton Pine* survived another two years of the war. Then, on 15 October 1942, when in a convoy bound for Halifax, she lost contact with the other ships in a storm and was never seen again. It was claimed she was sunk a day later by *U-704* in position 55° N 30° W.

Coincidental with the *Newton Pine*'s gun duel with her unidentified adversary, the *Sarastone* was riding out a howling gale in the Western Approaches. She was at the same time attempting to keep station in Convoy OG 47, bound from Milford Haven to Gibraltar. God and the weather were not on her side.

Built in 1929 and owned by Stone & Rolfe of Llanelli, the 2,473-ton *Sarastone* was a typical Welsh collier of her day. Small, sturdy and, like all overworked, ageing ships, she was subject to frequently recurring bouts of engine trouble. However, to Captain John Herbert and his crew of twenty-two the recalcitrant engine was a fact of life to be taken in its stride. There were worse things to worry about in the war.

When the *Sarastone* left Barry on 7 December 1940 she was loaded with 4,060 tons of coal, down to her marks and with precious little freeboard to keep at bay the North Atlantic in the depths of winter. In times of peace, she would have plodded down the Bristol Channel at her own pace and, with the exception of the unavoidable exposed crossing of the Bay of Biscay, prudently hugged the coast for much of the 1,100-mile passage to Gibraltar. Unfortunately, she was required to deliver herself into the hands of their Lordships at Milford Haven.

Having the protection of the convoy around him was of

some comfort to Captain Herbert, for the enemy's war against British shipping was at its height and the *Sarastone* was armed only with a 12-pounder and two light machine guns. But it was the route the convoy would follow that worried Herbert most. The southern exit from the Bristol Channel was now securely sealed off by British minesfields and OG 47 was to proceed around the north of Ireland and steam over 200 miles out into the North Atlantic before heading south. The *Sarastone* would be venturing into deep, unfamiliar waters and, for much of the time, would be far from a port of refuge should she get into difficulties.

John Herbert's worst fears were realized in the early hours of 20 December, when the *Sarastone* was 240 miles west of Cape Finisterre and labouring in the grip of a full gale. His chief engineer reported a serious defect in the port boiler, which would have to be shut down, leaving the ship with only half power. Herbert informed the convoy commodore of his predicament and was told to proceed independently, keeping a rendezvous with the convoy at noon on the 22nd, if possible. Five hours later the *Sarastone*, making only 2 knots in the heavy seas, had dropped astern and out of sight of the other ships. The deep laden collier, shipping green seas at every roll and barely maintaining steerage way, was alone.

Efforts were made to repair the leaking boiler but without the proper equipment, the *Sarastone*'s engineers could do little. Fortunately, within twenty-four hours, the weather moderated but by then the overstrained starboard boiler was also beginning to give trouble. Herbert decided to steer for Lisbon while he still had the means to make way through the water. Ignoring the proposed rendezvous with the convoy, he hauled over to the east, determined to close the Portuguese coast as soon as possible.

Shortly after settling down on her new course, the *Sarastone*'s wireless operator intercepted a message from the Admiralty reporting enemy submarine to the south of the ship and near to the rendezvous point given to Herbert by the convoy commodore. The Italian submarine *Moncenigo* was in fact already

s/s *Sarastone* 2473 GRT. Fought and won gun duel with Italian submarine *Mocenigo* off west coast of Spain 22 December 1940.

The Red Dragon Hits Back.

shadowing Convoy OG 47, and would attack it later that day.

The improvement in the weather continued and the 22nd dawned fine, with a light northwesterly wind barely rippling the sea and the horizon sharp and clear. Nursing her one remaining boiler, the *Sarastone* was averaging $5\frac{1}{2}$ knots and seemed sure of reaching Lisbon on the night of the 24th. The ill wind that had forced the ship to leave the convoy now blew fair for John Herbert and his crew. Christmas in neutral Portugal was a bonus they had not anticipated.

The first sign of trouble came near the end of the afternoon watch, when the Second Officer sighted what he thought to be a fishing boat on the starboard beam at about four miles. Being a cautious man, he called the Captain to the bridge. Herbert, squinting into the sun, which was low down on the starboard beam, was at once suspicious. The *Sarastone* was some 300 miles from the nearest land and in 600 fathoms of water, which was a most unlikely spot to encounter fishermen. As a first precaution, he ordered the Second Officer to call all hands on deck. A few minutes later, the dark object moved clear of the sun, and through his binoculars Herbert was not over surprised to see a submarine making towards his ship at speed.

The *Moncenigo*'s attack on Convoy OG 47 on the 21st had been something of a disappointment for her commander, Alberto Agostini. He had succeeded in sinking only the 1,253-ton Swedish steamer *Mangen*, before being chased off by the convoy escorts. Agostini was now on lookout for easier prey and, as he studied the slow-moving merchant ship through his binoculars, he was confident he had found it.

Herbert, still not sure if he was facing the enemy, took the only logical course open to him. He put his ship stern-on to the approaching submarine and ordered his gun's crew to close up on the 12-pounder mounted on the collier's poop.

The *Moncenigo*'s first shell, fired as the *Sarastone* was swinging to her helm, fell short, as did her subsequent shots. Herbert, realizing the limitations of his 12-pounder, ordered his gun-layer to hold his fire until the submarine was within 2,000 yards. At this range the *Sarastone*'s gun barked and the duel had begun.

Although the Italian submarine appeared to be using only one of her two deck guns and was firing hesitantly, shells began to land uncomfortably close to the Welsh ship as she ran away. Herbert concentrated on keeping his stern to the enemy and braced himself for the inevitable battering his ship must take. Then the impossible happened. The *Sarastone*'s 12-pounder, carefully laid by her gunlayer James O'Neill, scored a direct hit on the *Moncenigo*, sending smoke and flames shooting into the air. The submarine slewed round until she was beam-on and, to the accompaniment of ringing cheers from the collier's crew, a second shell from the 12-pounder slammed home.

The *Moncenigo* now appeared to be attempting to submerge and Herbert, his Celtic ire thoroughly aroused, ordered the bridge machine guns to open fire on the enemy. The range was too far for the light Hotchkiss guns but the 12-pounder continued to lob shells close to the submarine, whose efforts to submerge seemed unsuccessful. When the range had increased to 4,000 yards, Herbert ordered the 12-pounder to cease fire. The submarine was still on the surface and apparently stopped, with yellow smoke pouring from her after end. The *Sarastone* still had seven 12-pounder shells unfired but, mindful that his extraordinary luck might be stretched too far, Herbert resisted the impulse to close the enemy and finish her off. At 16.50 he stood his gun's crew down and set course for Lisbon.

The Portuguese capital was reached on the night of the 24th and John Herbert and his men were able to spend a well deserved Christmas in port. Repairs were carried out to the *Sarastone*'s boilers and she was eventually able to continue her voyage. In Gibraltar, she received 23 shells to replace those she had used up in her fight with the Italian but, such was the state of British ammunition stocks at this stage of the war, no cordite charges could be supplied for the shells. It was indeed fortunate for the plucky Welsh collier she did not fall in with the enemy on her howeward passage.

The *Moncenigo* did not sink but she was forced to retire to lick her wounds for a very long time. She was next heard of, under a new commander, in the Mediterranean in March 1942. Her continuing career was, however, as undistinguished as before. She accounted for only one ship, a 1,500-ton Frenchman, before being dispatched by US aircraft in a raid on Cagliari on 13 May 1943.

The *Sarastone*'s luck had run out eighteen months earlier. She was bombed and sunk when leaving the Spanish port of Huelva on 29 October 1941.

23

Requiem

The memories of the Second World War are now forty years-old and fading fast, but it will not go amiss to recall again the terrible losses Britain's Merchant Navy suffered in those dark days. In August 1945, when the conflict which had spread to the furthest reaches of the oceans at last drew to a close, the final reckoning was 2,426 British merchant ships of 11,331,933 tons sunk and 29,180 seamen lost. For almost three years, the outcome of the struggle had hung in the balance, needing only the merest wavering to tip the scales the wrong way. Between May 1940 and July 1941, sinkings were averaging 66 ocean-going ships a month, the climax being reached in May 1941, with 20 ships lost for every seven days that passed. It would then have been easy for Britain's merchant seamen, poorly paid and casually employed, to have adopted the attitude of many dockers, miners and shipyard workers who, conscious of their indispensability, regularly held their country to ransom using the now fashionable weapon of industrial action. If the merchant seamen, who were strictly speaking civilians, had refused to sail the ships – and the temptation to do just that must have been very great at times – then Britain would have gone under, for no nation can fight for long with stomachs empty and arsenals unstocked.

But despite the torpedoes, the shells, the mines, the bombs and the one in three prospect of a cold, unmarked grave, Britain's merchant seamen never once refused to leave port. It is sad to reflect that the bravery of the merchant seamen went almost unnoticed when the accolades were handed out. For the 29,180 who died, most of them denied even the dignity of a few yards of duck canvas, there remains only a forgotten memorial in an obscure corner of London's Tower Hill. That the men who died should not be remembered, except by those they left behind, is perhaps only another demonstration of human frailty. That the *raison d'être* of the sacrifice they made should be ignored is incomprehensible.

The British Commonwealth of Nations, as the Empire of yesterday is now called, once reached out to the four corners of the globe, covering over 13 million square miles, with a population of 450 million. Britain herself, with a large population and an economy based on manufacturing industry, was then wholly dependent on her merchant ships not only for her own sustenance but for communication and trade with her vast territories overseas. It is then not surprising that, at the beginning of this century, the Red Ensign flew over almost 50 per cent of the world's merchant shipping. In fact, such was the dominance of British ships that they carried over half the world's maritime trade in their bottoms.

The advent of the First World War highlighted the importance of this fleet, and sadly its vulnerability, when submarine warfare was for the first time introduced on a massive and ruthless scale. Britain did not starve, neither did she lack for arms and raw materials, but the price to her Merchant Navy was high, 2,479 ships and 14,879 seamen being lost. The damage was, however, quickly made good, replacement ships being built and the crews found to man them. Between the wars, in spite of the catastrophic depression of the early 1930s, British shipping, although never to achieve its dominance of the early days, held firm, and in 1939 was in a strong position once again to face up to a prolonged blockade. The necessity for a large British merchant fleet had been revealed for a second time.

The proving of the theory twice in the space of thirty years should have been a salutary lesson to the British people. This was apparently not so, or if the lesson was learnt it was not absorbed. When the Falklands mini-war came along, Britain's merchant fleet, for the first time in its long history, was found wanting. Committed at short notice to forming a retaliatory task force, the British government suffered the gross humiliation of having to charter in foreign merchant ships to make up the small, 49-ship support fleet. How was it that a nation which had fought and won the Battle of the Atlantic, sustaining at its height losses of 60 to 70 ships a month, had descended to such impotency?

Much of Britain's merchant tonnage lost in the Second World War was quickly replaced by ships mass-produced in the shipyards of the United States and Canada. These were all-welded ships of a very basic design, built primarily to see out the duration of the war and, perhaps, a year or two into the peace. Some did not even survive their first crossing of the Atlantic; many were sunk before the end of the war. By 1945, the .Merchant Navy was many millions of tons down on its pre-war strength. Some of the smaller shipping companies had been all but wiped out and the larger concerns were sadly depleted.

With the peace came the boom and, although Britain was near to economic bankruptcy and on the brink of losing her Empire, there was a rich harvest to be reaped in the maritime fields. The war-ravaged countries of Europe and the Far East were in desperate need of the goods and machinery to rebuild their shattered cities and industries. Within a few years, there was a world wide shortage of shipping, and British shipowners, ever with an eye to potential business, began to replenish their fleets.

By 1950, Britain owned nearly 25 per cent of the world's merchant shipping and looked set to regain her pre-eminence of the beginning of the century, when the Red Ensign dominated the trade routes and ports of the world. Over the next twenty-five years, while the uneasy peace of the nuclear deterrent reigned, the steady expansion continued until, in 1975, there were no less than 50 million tons of commercial shipping under the British flag. Then the bubble burst. Today, ten years on, Britain's merchant fleet stands at a mere 650 ships of 18 million tons and is shrinking at an ever accelerating rate. Conservative estimates predict a fleet of around 450 ships of $12\frac{1}{2}$ million tons by the end of 1986. A mighty fleet that Admiral Karl Dönitz and all his predatory U-boats failed to destroy is being thrown away, ship by ship, through complacency in the face of determined competition from outside.

Following the dissolution of the Empire, it was inevitable some of the newly indepedent nations would hanker after merchant fleets of their own. For any nation with a coastline, the desire to carry its own cargoes in its own ships is both understandable and good economic sense. The British, old masters of the Empire and unchallenged experts in the maritime field, were quick to recognize this. In the 1950s and 1960s, British aid, expertise and men were used to set up merchant fleets for India, Pakistan, Nigeria, Ghana and some of the East African countries. The success of these fleets was instant, for this was a time of unprecedented boom in shipping.

The new idea caught on and soon no developing maritime country was considered complete without its own fleet of merchant ships. India now has over 400 ships, which monopolize the trades which were once the prerogative of the shrinking British Merchant Navy. The Arab States of the Persian Gulf operate a 60-ship fleet of general cargo carriers which has all but excluded British ships from the lucrative Gulf trade. Taiwan, South Korea, Singapore, Bangladesh and Burma are only a few of the nations who have all joined enthusiastically in the business of the carriage of goods by sea. Most of these new fleets are heavily subsidized by their respective governments and their owners pay little or nothing in taxes. That many of the fleets are now run at a loss is of small concern to owners and governments, for when national prestige is at stake, profit takes a back seat. As a result Britain's completely unsubsidized and heavily taxed Merchant Navy is doomed to sink without trace.

While the British government is doggedly committed to a policy of free trade, the rest of the world takes a different view. The United States will not allow foreign ships into its coastal trade, nor will most of the EEC countries. The Soviet Union with a fleet of 4,000 state-owned and subsidized ships, moves virtually all its own cargo, coastal and deep-sea. On the Indian sub-continent, in Asia and in Africa political pressure is used to secure national cargoes for national flag ships. And all the while, Britain, for centuries the dominant sea power of the world, stubbornly refuses to offer any form of economic or political protection to its dwindling merchant fleet.

Subsidization and protectionism apart, by far the greatest threat to British commercial shipping is the flag of convenience; the safe haven for the unscrupulous shipowner looking for a quick return on his money, with no tax to be paid, no allegiance to be owed and precious few rules to adhere to. Year after year, casualty figures prove the majority of flag of convenience ships are poorly manned, equipped and maintained. Yet they continue to operate, apparently free from interference by the bodies which supposedly police the world's commercial shipping. As a direct result of the low freights they are able to offer, these same ships rarely lack cargoes and are often to be seen plying the seas loaded well below their deliberately rust-streaked Plimsoll marks. Incredible though it may seem, these latter-day freebooters are, in most cases, able to obtain, without difficulty, full insurance cover for their ships and cargoes.

The situation has now become so grave that British ship-owners having cargo to move find it cheaper to charter in foreign tonnage, thereby condemning their own ships to the slow death of the lay-by berth. The inevitable happens. British ships, made redundant through high running costs, are sold to eagerly awaiting foreign buyers as going concerns. With a very short space of time, these ships are back at sea, under a new flag, often in the same trade, lifting the same cargoes and in direct competition with their previous British owners. Operated on the cheap and with little thought for safety, their profitability is assured. Meanwhile, the British shipowner is forced to turn his shareholder's money to better uses. One by one, British shipping companies, some of them household names in the maritime world for over a hundred years, have been forced to shut up shop for ever. In consequence, two-thirds of Britain's considerable maritime trade is now carried in foreign bottoms.

What of the fleet of the Red Dragon? Where are the plodding *Sarastones*, the proud *St Essylts* and the gallant *Lady Glanelys* of today? As I write, the great Reardon Smith Line, seventy-three years in Welsh shipping, has sold its last ship and gone into liquidation. Evan Thomas, Radcliffe & Co., 101 years in the business and reduced in the end to the coastal trade, bowed out in 1983. Evans & Reid went in the same year. South American Saint, Tatems, Constants, Tempus and all those once evocative names faded in the 1960s and 1970s never to return. The port of Cardiff, which in 1910 was home to 369 deep-sea ships, now has only nine vessels registered in the port. Newport has only two ships on its books, while Swansea has none. The fleet of the Red Dragon, which gave so many ships and so many men in two wars that Welshmen might continue to live in freedom, is no more. Oswald Swayne, John Reardon Smith, Ebenezer Williams, Henry Isaac and all the others unnamed died in vain, for the people of Wales have long forgotten their maritime heritage.

A succession of British governments, for reasons of dogma or political necessity, has been prepared to pour money into the bottomless coffers of inefficient, overmanned, uneconomical nationalized industries. It seems no price has been too high in order to gain some political advantage. Yet, even in the light of the Falklands experience, there is still no move to offer succour to a dying British Merchant Navy. Britain is now the only western maritime nation totally without govern-mental support, in cash or in kind, for its merchant shipping. Should she ever become engaged in a major war again, her umbilical cord to the warehouses of the outside world would be slashed through in the opening weeks of the conflict, leaving her people faced with the choice of abject surrender or a slow death in isolation.

Bibliography

Appleyard, H. S. & Heaton, P. M., *The Baron Glanely of St. Fagans & W. J. Tatem Ltd* (World Ship Society, Kendall n.d.).

Beaver, Paul, *U-Boats in the Atlantic* (Patrick Stephens, Cambridge, 1979).

Brown, Anthony Cave, *Bodyguard of Lies* (W. H. Allen, London, 1977).

Bucheim, Lothar-Gunther, *U-Boat War* (Collins, London, 1978).

Churchill, W. S., *The Second World War* (Cassel & Co. Ltd., London, 1948–52).

Costello & Hughes, *The Battle of the Atlantic* (Collins, London, 1977).

Cremer, Peter, *U-333* (The Bodley Head, London, 1984).

Heaton, P. M., *Reardon Smith Line* (P. M. Heaton, Pontypool, 1984).

HMSO, *British Vessels Lost at Sea 1939–45* (HMSO, London, 1947).

— *Merchantmen at War* (HMSO, London, 1944).

Hocking, Charles, *Dictionary of Disasters at Sea During the Age of Steam 1824–1962* (Lloyd's Register of Shipping, London, n.d.).

Jenkins, J. Geraint, *Evan Thomas Radcliffe* (National Museum of Wales, Cardiff, 1982).

National Museum of Wales, *The Maritime Heritage of Dyfed* (National Museum of Wales, Cardiff, 1982).

Rohwer, Jurgen, *Axis Submarine Successes 1939–1945* (Patrick Stephens, Cambridge, 1983).

Roskill, Captain S. W., *The War at Sea* (HMSO, London, 1954–61).

Woon, Basil, *Atlantic Front* (Peter Davies, London 1941).

The *Western Mail*, (Cardiff 1939–45).

Index

Index 201